KHALI

# Eyes
## on GAZA

## Witnessing
## Annihilation

with art by
Mohammad
Sabaaneh

STREET NOISE BOOKS　•　BROOKLYN, NEW YORK

*This book is dedicated to all the victims*
*Departed, alive, and barely living*
*Of Nakbas new, old, and ongoing*

ISBN 978-1951-491-41-3

Cover art by Mohammad Sabaaneh

Printed in the U.S.

9 8 7 6 5 4 3 2 1

First Edition

# TABLE OF CONTENTS

**Introduction: Olives and Time**      **1**

**Part I**   For Ali & Edward      **15**

Before Day 1   Gaza As Panopticon      17

Day 7   On Terrorists and Freedom Fighters      21

Day 10   Living on Borrowed Time      29

Day 16   Gaza 2.0: The First Digital Genocide      36

Day 34   An Ode to Anaam      43

Day 47   Don't Call it a Ceasefire      48

**Part II**   For Reem & Hind      **53**

Day 50   The Next Sinister Stage of Ethnic Cleansing      55

Day 51   The Soul of My Soul      60

Day 60   What About the Men?      64

Day 64   Meta vs. Palestine      73

Day 72   No Christmas in Gaza      78

Day 108   Motaz, Our Brother from Gaza      82

Day 136   Aaron Bushnell and the Rage Within      89

Day 140   Man on Fire      94

**Part III**   For Aaron & Issam      **101**

Day 152   A Ramadan Starved By Genocide      103

Day 225   Disintegration      108

Day 232   Machine Dreams, Digital Nightmares      112

Day 248   Finding Justice in Cape Town      119

Day 271   Searching for Edward      125

Day 294   The People's Champ      131

Day 348   When Phones are Bombs      137

**Conclusion: Old Body, New Mind**      **147**

Endnotes      153

## Introduction

## Olives and Time

*"Gaza is devoted to rejection, hunger and rejection, thirst and rejection, displacement and rejection, torture and rejection, siege and rejection, death and rejection."*
— *Silence in Gaza*, Mahmoud Darwish[1]

On October 8th, 2023, Gaza was silent no more.

It exploded with a sound never heard before. Then in the weeks that followed, it spiraled into a theater of "death and rejection" that not even Mahmoud Darwish could foresee.[2] And few of us could have anticipated the scope it would take in the days and weeks to come.

The pace of change was furious, with the fate of more than two million people teetering between military siege and mass slaughter. The horrific attacks north of its border claimed the lives of approximately 1200 Israelis, marking the greatest attack on Israeli soil and a new era in the crisis. October 7th, referred to as "Black Saturday" in Israel, opened the floodgates of rage on Gaza, and in the downward spiral of genocide that followed forever changed its fate.[3]

The scale of destruction was prolific, as was the severity of military violence. The death toll rose rapidly as Israeli bombs and munitions took aim indiscriminately in Gaza, dropping dumb bombs that crushed homes and killed dozens to hundreds on a nearly daily basis. The imprecision of the attacks combined with the concentration of the people in Gaza, the third most densely populated place in the world, spelled limitless slaughter and unimaginable destruction, and accelerated an ethnic cleansing project made possible by the "shared rage" of unhinged militarism and societal zeal for vengeance within Israeli society after October 7th.[4] The horrors that followed were *war crimes of passion*, pursued by a Benjamin Netanyahu-led government that now had carte blanche to pummel Gaza and punish all of its inhabitants. Their agenda of collective punishment was on full display for the world to see, on television and mobile screens, marking days of unseen rage that sunk into uncut genocide.

Mass death and displacement, siege and starvation did not stop. Days blended into weeks, and weeks blurred into months. The slow march of ethnic cleansing that preceded October 7th raced forward with blinding speed, as the right-wing government's project of expanding Israeli military control was achieved in days, expediting its vision of cleansing Gaza of its Palestinian population. The first day of the siege foreshadowed the violence to come, a prolonged bombing campaign that would mercilessly fall on the people of Gaza. The Western media spun coverage that facilitated Netanyahu's aggression, portraying the whole of Gaza as terrorist sympathizers and Hamas proxies in order to justify the disproportionate and unhinged onslaught. Children were not innocents, but human shields, and everyday residents of the Strip considered collateral damage post-mortem.

The victims were made into villains, all of them, as bombs fell atop their heads. The words of Malcolm X rushed into my head as I took in the propaganda portrayed by legacy media outlets in the United States: "If you're not careful, the newspapers will have you hating the people who are being oppressed, and loving the people who are doing the oppressing."

Struck by the relevance, I crafted an Instagram post showcasing the ruins of the initial bombing campaign and using those words of Malcolm X to mark the moment and the spot. And this post instantly went viral.[5] As a child of the Lebanese Civil War and scholar shaped by the post-9/11 War on Terror, I knew what was to come, and even more menacingly, I felt the crippling grip of fear come over friends of mine in Gaza and throughout the region. However, I could not even imagine the devastation that would be wrought on Gaza and its people, and those targeted by airstrikes and deadly forms of militarized technology, while the horror of expanding war threatened to spread beyond the borders of the Strip.

Like billions around the world, far from the belly of bombs in Gaza, my world was undone and enveloped by this genocide. The grey panoramas of destroyed streets and squares that I saw across screens and timelines brought back memories from my childhood of the shattered landscapes of a war-torn Beirut.

The faces and figures of this genocide felt intimately familiar, compelling me toward some form of action, whatever I could take on. As days passed, friends and family members were killed. Individuals I had developed relationships with in-person and online went missing for long stretches, only later to be counted among the "missing" people added to a skyrocketing death toll. Emergent new voices of journalists rose from the rubble of genocide to tell the story from the very soil where their family members were slain. The world witnessed genocide unfold with unprecedented clarity and color, between digital screens and military sieges. It pulled us in as participants mobilized into advocacy and parties moved into action.

As I writer, I found sanity and safe haven through the written word. On

social media platforms I provided rolling and real-time analysis of major events, crafting posts on Instagram that amplified the voices of those on the ground, or gave directives as a law scholar attempting to provide guidance. Through articles and lectures, interviews and blogs, I struggled to piece together strings of sanity to make sense of a senseless impasse, to dissect the absurd reality of *genocide* unfolding before my eyes; before all of our eyes. The very word *genocide*—a technical and legal term—became the subject of debate and even controversy, as proponents of the Israeli siege and those holding adjacent views dismissed the applicability of the indictment.[6]

However, the mounting death toll, macabre scenes of decimation, and statistical surge of catastrophic famine, limbless children, and listless attempts to stop the horror affirmed what the world already knew. As the words of Netanyahu, Itamar Ben-Gvir, Bezalel Smotrich, and other Israeli leaders rang with genocidal intent, the genocidal actions unfolding in Gaza were shared online, conveying to global audiences what legacy media had conspired to keep hidden.

I wrote and posted, amplified and spoke up, day in and day out, out of both principled obligation and existential need. Gaza was silent no more, so neither could we be.

But it was not enough. It never felt like enough. Despite how much I wrote and spoke, the images and stories of genocide emanating from Gaza made everything feel short, shallow, and incomplete. I never set foot in Gaza, but the people I interacted with daily on the ground, combined with the reels of horror privately delivered to me from firsthand accounts, created a paradox of fuel and debilitation, power and pacification; I was stuck inside that crucible and the Catch-22 of a catastrophe I could not shake off. And from which I could not remove myself despite my best efforts.

But words brought catharsis. The written word, combining real-time feeling with rolling analysis and the structure of sentences, brought a veneer of order to a world that had lost every semblance of it. Writing brought solace as I lost myself in the ephemeral havens of shelter created by the belief that what I was doing, what I was writing, would have some impact. That it could make some change. So, I wrote each day of this genocide, with the purpose of memorializing a human catastrophe that could not be erased, that I was determined would not be forgotten despite the repeated conspiracy to deny, dismiss, and eventually bury it. As a scholar, I knew the trudging order of imperial history all too well, and raised my pen rebelliously against its march. This, despite the degree of dehumanization in Gaza and the scale of erasure achieved by the Netanyahu regime, could not be erased from history, and would not be buried under the rubble of Western and white supremacist texts that vindicated the villains and killed the victims twice – on the killing fields and pages of his-story.

As the days rolled onward and the images of genocide grew bleaker, I found strength in the words of intellectual predecessors who'd encountered kindred human catastrophes. I realized that my station, as a law professor and scholar, came with an obligation. A responsibility that grew weightier at the silence of my academic colleagues in law and other disciplines. The risks

associated with speaking out on Gaza silenced them, just as the incentives of turning a blind eye to a genocide kept me—against my best interests—wide awake, livid, and loud. What I witnessed moved me to remain active, as a documentarian of genocide, on digital platforms where doomscrolling dystopic images and evidence of genocide marshalled the world into action.

Gaza was at the mercy of Netanyahu. This was facilitated by the Strip's multidimensional reliance on Israel, or what Marc Lamont Hill and Michael Plitnick call "the physical ghettoization," born from the Camp David Accords of 1978. In *Except for Palestine*, Hill and Plitnick observe, "As a result of its encirclement, Gaza became dramatically more reliant on Israel in fundamental ways. All of its infrastructure—electricity, water, and trade—was now inextricably dependent on Israel, and there was no way for the people of Gaza to develop any alternative."[7] This was on stunning and sobering display during the genocide, as Netanyahu cut off water pipelines into Gaza, disrupted power and electricity in line with military objectives, and instituted blockades to starve millions. This signaled a sobering reality: the genocide did not begin on

October 8th; the infrastructure and agenda were firmly in place for decades before that date. What has unfolded since was its acceleration, and this finally stopped the world in its tracks to see the horrors that the people of Gaza endured for far too long.

Over the course of the days and months, as I wrote the pieces that would coalesce into this book, the theatre of absolute horror was nonstop. Hundreds of mosques were destroyed; every single college and university in Gaza bombed into oblivion; hospitals and the entire medical infrastructure were wiped off the face of the earth; humanitarian squads were targeted; and the primary relief agency, the United Nations Relief and Works Association (UNRWA), was strategically demonized to further the emaciation of the people of Gaza.[8] Not to mention the killing, the nonstop killing, which made its way from the soil of the Strip to the dystopian screens held tightly in our hands. All eyes were on Gaza, and we all became witnesses to its annihilation.

We would never be the same. Forever turned around by a genocide that seared grim images in our minds of gruesomely disfigured children; mourning mothers holding their dead daughters in white sheets; and hysterical fa-thers digging into the rubble for lost sons they would never find. These ghastly and scarring images, and many more were burned into our memories as the portal of our eyes absorbed them from new Orwellian telescreens tethered to our bodies; attached to our palms like postmodern appendages.

"The people of Gaza live[d] in a situation much too precarious to be ignored" before October 7th.[9] But after it, precarity and peril spiraled into hell on earth. As a child reared in the Lebanese Civil War that ushered in the very same Israeli incursions and airstrikes, I could empathize fully with those Gazans on the ground. As a scholar of law and Islamophobia, I understood intimately how the absence of the former and the impact of the latter would arm Israel with a license to inflict unrestrained violence on Gaza. More than just speak up, I had to write and *right*, activities that felt identical within that widening ring of fire of genocide.

"Writing, righting, and rioting" through word encompassed far more than speaking out in the moment. Or writing against imperial power in the now.[10] Speaking out against genocide should not be just reactive but must be productive. *Rewriting* accounts of events in Gaza, as they unfolded, was a form of "rioting" in and of itself. Knowledge production, in fact, is a lasting form of resistance and rebellion countering the hegemonic distortion of history that plagues my people, and subaltern people of every complexion or confes-sion. I knew, only days into the genocide, that the most salient contribution I could make to the people of Gaza (and then Lebanon) was writing history as it unfolded, by which I could inject hope in young minds and dissident voices searching for the rule of law in a world that selectively applied it.

The African proverb popularized by Chinua Achebe took hold of me, echoing again and again in my mind as I absorbed the daily events of geno-cide. "Until the lions have their own historians, history of the hunt will always glorify the hunter."[11] *Things fall apart*, and the scale of disintegration in Gaza and then in Lebanon brought new dystopian meaning to those words. That lofty title activated an urgency to bring new word to its inherent call toward action; toward knowledge production from the bottom.[12] But history, when written from the prism of the subaltern and the pens of lions, possessed the power to reimagine, then reconstruct, and finally remake. And during the daily haze and existential maze of genocide, writing was often the only thing that made me feel normal. Even more, it became the lasting thing that made me *feel*. Feeling again was what made sense of living, and writing brought raw feeling to rise up against the march of nihilism ushered in by genocide.

––––––––––

As a child, I remember walking through the aisleways of grocery stores with my late father. The Lebanese Civil War had flung us back to Michigan, to a Midwestern town where a myriad of Arab populations took refuge and re-built their lives. And what were routine trips for groceries then, have become treasured moments of reflection today. My father, always the maverick, would pick and eat from the nuts and fruits as he pushed his grocery cart forward. His favorite stop was the olive bar – a station on the margins of the market where an eclectic mosaic of olives, ranging in hue from green to black to brown, glistened and summoned him in.

That was his favorite stop in the market. And over time, it became mine as well. Around the olive station, with a plastic container in hand, my fa-ther would walk around and pick olives from the array. What were samples evolved into stories, evoking nostalgia and longing, tales with the taste of re-gret, loss, and at times, hope. "These remind of me home," he uttered one day, picking from the medley of olives mixed with peppers and carrots. He handed me one, then reflected upon his childhood in that south Lebanon town, Bint Jbiel, only a stone's throw from the border that Balfour and other colonial conspirators drew in the soil. A son of the *mountain's daughter*, my fa-ther Ali, flung far from it by old world woes and new world wars.[13]

"I used to pick these same olives from our own trees," he reflected as his mouth curled into a faint smile. He seldom smiled around us, but even though

I was a child, I knew what those upwardly curved lips signaled. I knew that my father, who had dropped out of school as a child and then migrated north to Beirut to support his family, romanticized his past and felt deeply connected to where he was from. The war in Lebanon broke him, while life in America left him adrift inside the foreign lines of new lands, lost time, and crushing space. This was his grand narrative, which on the worst days morphed into a curse that troubled both him and the family he struggled to keep and keep whole.

My father was illiterate. But his reflections around the olive bar and beyond affirmed that he understood the importance of history. The vitality of the written word to a people dispossessed of land and displaced entirely from the historical record. "There were also trees on the other side of where the border is today. There was no border then. We would walk and pick from those Palestinian trees and play with our friends," he continued, filling the container with the very olives he sampled from; the very olives that transported him back to where he belonged, where he always wanted to be.

"Back then, we were all the same. But today, we are all Palestinian." I did not know what he meant then, as a ten-year-old child of war now living in Detroit. But I came to know it as I aged, as I learned about my father's familial roots in Palestinian villages, his childhood travels selling wares and whatever he could, his solidarity with Palestinian refugees exiled in Lebanon, his financing of Palestinian musicians, and his deeply rooted support of the Palestinian cause. My father was not formally educated and could not write or read in his native tongue, and his English vocabulary was limited to about fifteen or twenty words that he picked from to piece together functional sentences. But his knowledge of politics was extensive, and his mastery of its history seemed to rival any formally trained scholar. I soaked in everything he shared with me, and later understood the importance of learning at the foot of an illiterate scholar short on formal education but rich in wisdom. While I came to love the company of books, my father preferred the company of people, and he would sit at cafes with émigrés from Iraq, Yemen, Palestine, Syria, and other accosted points of the region, learning about their worlds while he shared worlds of his own.

Those olive trees he loved symbolized the land of Palestine, and still today stand as the archetypal emblems of indigeneity and survival. These trees are resilient, firmly rooted across Palestinian villages, south Lebanon, and adjacent lands once undivided from its soil and society. The olives it spawns are its children, no matter how far gone they are from its roots. Neither distance nor time could change that fact, could erase the nativity of a people exiled. These olive trees predate the postcolonial borders that spawned disparate nation states and divided peoples. They precede the wars and wounds inflicted by them, and preexist the genocide ravaging the people of Gaza today.

My father, Abu Khaled, passed away many years ago. I often wonder what words he would share about this genocide, this human catastrophe that began well before October 7th of 2024. As the days of the siege roll onward, I reflect on those formative strolls around the olive bar. And during those elusive nights of sleep, I return to the olive bar and I speak to my father about unfolding events as he pushes his cart around it. Those olives he loved so much embody a cause that supersedes man-made boundaries and their imperial hold on time. Those olive trees and the olives they birth embody who we were in past times, and after the unmaking of our lands, who we will strive to be again.

This book is a medley of reflections crafted during the surreal stretch of genocide. We have a responsibility to take back history from the hands of those conspiring to distort it, and us along with it. This is a native son's quest to pen the eloquent words my illiterate father could only speak, during this time when I need to hear them most.

My father was no intellectual, not by formal definition at least. But his zeal for justice, and his defense of the dignity of Palestinians, raised my consciousness and commitment to writing the words he was unable to.

An *intellectual*, I discovered at a young age, is defined more by courage than credentials. Edward Said's articulation of the role and responsibility of the intellectual resonates more deeply with me as catastrophes unfold, and as the voices of scholars and professors remain confined to ivory towers. Especially as the juxtaposed memories of war-torn Beirut blur with the real-time images of catastrophe in Gaza and in Lebanon, Said's words are commands that ring with urgency and the immediate need of action: "It is a spirit of opposition, rather than in accommodation, that grips me because the romance, the interest, the challenge of intellectual life is to be found in dissent against the status quo at a time when the struggle on behalf of underrepresented and disadvantaged groups seems so unfairly weighted against them."[14]

And in Gaza that struggle is now falling so violently atop them in the forms of missiles and bombs, catastrophic famine and crushing rubble.

Both my father Ali and Edward are gone. But it is during these times, this genocide, when their words matter most. When I hear them most clearly, as dictates to write; and as dictates to fight. From the roots of the trees native to lands that knew no boundary before Balfour or Sykes-Picot, long before English and Frenchmen stepped foot atop its soil to divide our people and spawn our struggle.

The passages you will read in the coming pages rise from roots planted long before the genocide in Gaza. The art accompanying the words was drawn by a Palestinian artist who is seeded in the land, and who brings firsthand images to the words. Essays and art are in harmony, reaching across old colonial borders and beyond new digital orders, to memorialize the annihilation of a people, *our people*.

Against the barriers of foes old and new, we pray, this book will be passed on like olives. Olives that, *inshallah*, will nourish the courage to keep on writing, righting, and fighting. We are all witnesses to the annihilation of Gaza. And like olive trees scattered across those disputed lands and decimated pasts, we must rise up against military weapons and imperial prisons that conspire to uproot indigenous truths today and tomorrow.

# Part I

For Ali & Edward

## Gaza As Panopticon

*"To divide, deploy, schematize, tabulate, index, and record
everything in sight (and out of sight)."*
— Edward Said, *Orientalism*[15]

For the first-time voyeur, Gaza appears to be a narrow slice of heaven outside the gates of the Holy Land. A place where palm trees reach high for bright skies above, with outstretched beaches lining the twenty-five miles of land kissing the bright blue sea of the Mediterranean.

But Gaza is anything but paradise. It is hell for two million captives.[16] An "open air prison," as many call it, where airstrikes and massacres strip bare the tropical veneer of palm trees and pristine beaches.

More than just a prison, Gaza is the *perfect* type of prison. Examining it as such through Jeremy Bentham's template of the "Panopticon" is instructive for purposes of understanding the total state of surveillance that spiraled into siege following October 7th, 2023.[17] By framing Gaza as a 148-square-mile prison made by a hyper-militarized Israeli state fearing the hypermasculine threat within it, the gendered dialectic that animates the siege is fully understood.

In Gaza, Israel acts as state overseer and societal warden and sees and controls everything. The Panopticon motif reveals how "the ensemble of punishment, discipline, and control" make Gaza a repressive "society of subjugation,"[18] a place where a foreign power controls virtually every element of life. A "schematized" plot of land made of material checkpoints manned by soldiers, and digital boundaries tracked by hovering drones and movable data.[19] With the metaphoric watchtower everywhere in Gaza, the "Israeli gaze" affixes itself on every single body and movement within the Strip, monitoring it in line with the mandate of occupation and subjugation.[20]

The subjugation of Gaza spans decades. Israel formally passed on *control* over Gaza to the PLO in 1994 but used the outfit as a proxy to administer its own rule. The Israeli government disarmed Gaza of a standalone military, denied it an airport, and surveilled its boundaries with manned checkpoints increasingly monitoring everyone who went out and came in. Like any prison, escape is virtually impossible, and surveillance is a passive mode of control that can abruptly turn into punishment at the slightest sign of transgression.

Again, the Israeli gaze is perpetually on the Gazan body, both corporeal and land. This was a hyper-masculine gaze, not necessarily in the form of biological sex, but in what Judith Butler calls the "performance" of muscular control over every specter of Gazan life. Every Gazan was given an orange (then blue) identity card by Israel, which noted their comings and goings. Within the Panopticon of Gaza, the all-seeing Israeli state gaze controls the space and time of its Palestinian residents. Sociologist Elia Zuriek observes,

> *The temporality of space is thus shaped by a daily routine of occupation in which Palestinians are subjected to endless waiting and detours, whether on the road, at work, or in establishing stable relations – so much so that as the Israeli journalist Amira Hass has remarked, it amounts to a "theft of time".[21]*

Palestinians are "doing time" simply by living in Gaza. And the men, women, and children followed by digital tracking, intrusive checkpoints, and military discipline externalized by the State of Israel.

In line with the Foucauldian concept of Panopticism, the feeling of always being monitored disciplines Gazans to obey, surrender, and avoid any activity that could be interpreted as resistance.[22] Thus, Gazans *internalize* that discipline through strict obedience, which is *externalized* by War on Terror policies and indictments enforced upon them for acts of (perceived) transgression, or no transgression at all. Consequently, Gazans become "principals of their own subjugation" and "agents of their own confinement" by training themselves to avoid activity that signals disobedience, let alone terrorism.[23]

But the Israeli gaze does not merely confine Gazans, it controls every one of its lifelines. It is vital to understand that this Panoptic setup of Gaza enabled the scale of collective punishment that followed October 7th. In essence, Gaza's complete reliance on Israel creates an umbilical cord where virtually every dimension of Gazan life was dependent on the Israeli state. In *Except for Palestine*, Marc Lamont Hill and Mitchell Plitnick observe, "All its infrastructure—electricity, water, trade—was now inextricably dependent on Israel, and there was no way for the people of Gaza to develop any alternative . . . The effects of measures that were taken in the 1990s to improve economic conditions for the people of Gaza . . . were blunted by the tight Israeli controls that were exercised over them."[24]

Israeli omniscience and control over Gaza expedited the military and infrastructural decimation that unfolded in the days after October 7th. Further, its control over water supply, delivery of aid, and travel deepened suffering on the ground. As in a prison, the Israeli state could reflexively punish its captives en masse, deny them food, water, medical attention, and other forms of vital aid through unilateral closures and absolute control of the Gaza borders.[25]

Certainly, these denials violate the legal thresholds of the 8th Amendment in the U.S., as well as protections for Israeli prisoners within its territory.[26] But Gaza was a prison full of *subjects*, not citizens. A Panopticon composed of captives, not civilians, whose lives were reduced by an Israeli gaze that saw and surveilled them through the lens of terrorism. The presumption of terrorism swallows all privacy in Gaza, which has been engineered into a "total surveillance society" built on the back of Palestinian men, or *boogiemen*, residing in Gaza: the besieged belly of terror where captivity could, at any second, spiral into genocide. A fate engineered more by architecture before October 7th than the onslaught in the dark days that followed.

## On Terrorists and Freedom Fighters

*"My only consolation is that periods of colonization pass, that nations sleep only for a time, and that peoples remain."*
— Aimé Césaire[27]

*Journalist: The law's often inconvenient, Colonel.*

*Colonel Mathieu: And those who explode bombs in public places, do they respect the law perhaps?*
— The Battle of Algiers[28]

Reality is darker theatre than fiction. Hollywood studios cannot conjure or curate the horror that unfolded in Gaza in the days after October 7th, where the body parts of children were scattered across playgrounds, where civilians were rounded up and then slaughtered seconds later after the fall of another airstrike. I stumbled through life during the first days of Israel's siege of Gaza, scrambling through the reels of genocidal reality intruding my screens and the scenes of bygone films with renewed meaning. Prepping for my course on Islamophobia and the Law, I revisited the French occupation of Algeria, and the sublime grassroots resistance it gave rise to.

The landmark film, *The Battle of Algiers*, brought the stunning drama of the Algerian Revolution to screens everywhere. From the winding walkways of the Casbah to the legions of foreign soldiers whirling through them, the film captured the imperial horror of the effect of 132 years of French occupation. Long after the savagery of French colonization in Algeria, the film serves as a stunning metanarrative for grassroots resistance, and the push for self-determination in Palestine that remains—even during the thick of genocide.

On the silver screen, the world finally saw and understood the Algerians for who they were: a people fighting for their independence with everything they had. Through the director's subaltern lens, the film exposed the unhinged "barbarism" that loomed underneath the pristine uniform of "civilization" adorned and advanced by the colonial French. The roles of the "terrorist" and "freedom fighter" were cinematically retold, reversing the weight of law and its imprint on colonial history. Those terms, even more today, are imbued with more racial than legal meaning, as the justification of collective punishment of Gaza illustrates.

As the director Gillo Pontecorvo showed and Jean-Paul Sartre wrote: "When despair drove [the Algerians] to revolt, these subhumans either had to perish or assert their humanity against us: they rejected all our values, our culture, our supposed superiority."[29] They chose to assert their humanity through acts of resistance and revolution. Against the highest odds, and one of the world's most advanced armies, Algerians mounted resistance after en-

during decades of mourning for massacre after massacre.

The film still, nearly six decades later, rises as revolutionary theatre in relation to events in Gaza. It masterfully recreates the asymmetrical battle between the indigenous Algerians, most powerfully the women, who rooted anything and everything in the loins of the land they loved merely to survive the French. Only that brand of love, *indigenous love*, could scale odds stacked so heavily against them. They faced legions of colonial soldiers brandishing the most modern weaponry, and the blow of imperial laws crafted to steal their rightful claim of the soil that sheltered their ancestors and nourished their fight.

As *The Battle of Algiers* made clear, the law is often the colonizer's first front of attack. Lawfare typically precedes warfare. Through word, law is used to strip the natural claim of self-governance deriving from indigeneity, and then swiftly unravels the humanity of those resisting with their bodies and their being. Law enables the colonial power and its foot soldiers to carry the fight within the most intimate quarters of the natives' homes. And then,

law labels any righteous resistance against it as "terrorism," whether in the alleyways of Algerian squares or the occupied hearts of Gazan streets.

The charge of terrorism, per its modern War on Terror deployment and earlier use, is crafted deliberately along lines of race, religion, and geopolitical interests, as illustrated by the kindred realities unfolding in the Casbah then, and in accosted squares of Kyiv and Rafah today.[30]

Law converts that very absurdity—that a foreign force holds possessory rights over a native's home—into the manmade fiat of manifest destiny. Brutal soldiers invoked this legal authority crafted by foreign men in distant capitals and cruelly imposed it on natives as their new fate. This is the law's cardinal function in settler colonial states like America and imperial experiments such as Algeria — to delegitimize self-determination and dehumanize those who resist.

"*The rule of law?*" Aimé Césaire asks rhetorically: "I look around and wherever there are colonizers and the colonized face to face, I see force, brutality, cruelty, sadism, conflict," and as Gaza stands as a living case study, genocide.[31] Law, in this sense, is an imperial instrument, molded and maneuvered to advance the interests of those who hold power, and who will use that power to translate authoritative law into ominous violence. As law scholar Ian Haney Lopez observes, "Law is one of the most powerful mechanisms by which any society creates, defines, and regulates itself."[32] But even more, law is an instrument that is wielded by imperial and oppressive nations as a blunt instrument from within and without. Law becomes most lethal when it envisions its targets as objects of conquest rather than subjects of patronage.

The discourse between the journalist in *The Battle of Algiers* and Lieutenant Colonel Philippe Mathieu illustrates this imperial expedience of law, or convenience, in vivid display. Mathieu is the cinematic embodiment of the steely French entitlement driving its colonial obsession with Algeria. With regard to Ukraine, the French in the movie stand as a telling archetype for the arrogant authoritarianism of President Vladimir Putin, whose obsession with power is wed to a kindred nostalgia of Soviet regional and global hegemony. This discourse about law and power, imperialism and indigeneity is built upon a fundamental conception of freedom fighters and terrorists—a timeless dialectic that screams from the screens as it did in *The Battle of Algiers*.

Political reality, for many, inspires the best cinema. In a world marred by two decades of a global War on Terror, racial reckoning, and cold wars of the past thawing which restored bygone geopolitical rivalries, modern reality is as gripping as fiction. *Terrorism* has taken on a pointed racial and religious form. Arabs and Muslims, transnationally, have been "raced" as terrorists as a consequence of this American-led crusade.[33] Their faith is conflated with extremism and their portrayal in American media and law is constructed based on that conflation. As American law scholar Caroline Mala Corbin aptly puts, "terrorists are always Muslim but never white."[34]

Legitimizing this indictment, global War on Terror law and propaganda have indelibly affirmed this connection. They obscure the humanity of Muslims in favor of a political visage that enables policing and prosecution in America, and military persecution and mass punishment abroad. This

occurs even in lands where Muslims—like the Algerian women and men in Gilo Pontecorvo's classic film, or Palestinians in Gaza—are doing anything to stay alive. *Seeing* them as terrorists facilitates the *unseeing* of them for what they rightfully are: freedom fighters struggling for the same dignity that Ukrainians, taking arms in the midst of impending conquest, clench onto in the face of imposing Russian aggression.

The force of imperial law, that strips the land from its rightful holders and simultaneously brands them as inferior or inhuman, is most effective when driven by a "racialized" frame.[35] Postcolonial thinkers of eras past, most trenchantly Césaire, Frantz Fanon, and Edward Said, revealed how the accompanying hand of racism expedited the plunder of nonwhite peoples.

Today, critical race theorists emphatically and incessantly affirm racism's centrality to law, against the political and legal tidal wave that seeks to disfigure and discredit it.[36] There is perhaps no theatre of law where the salience of race is on fuller display than the War on Terror, where the unabashed demonization of Muslims remains politically palatable and culturally pervasive. Islamophobia stands as a final bastion of acceptable and rewarded bigotry. This is especially apparent in the United States, and a globalized world remade through a War on Terror lens over the last twenty-three years. The colors of freedom and terror are intimately tethered to the world order remade by the War on Terror. Muslims are "presumptive terrorists," a charge levied on account of race, religion, and *realpolitik*, even when acting as freedom fighters.[37]

A distant, yet kindred campaign for self-determination reinforced the power of this indictment, with a racial design as its marrow. It took form in Europe, beginning on February 24, 2022, when Russian missiles rained down on the Ukraine, foreshadowing the thunderous military storm seeking to restore reign over the former Soviet colony.

The formidable Russian army rushing in from the east was universally branded imperialist, while Ukrainians, from the highest rungs of political office to the deepest roots of lay society, were globally celebrated as freedom fighters. Ukrainians embodied the indigenous fight of Algerians then, or Palestinians today, against a global military power intent on crushing their hearts, homes, and everything they love beyond and in between.

Unlike the accusations leveled at their Palestinian counterparts striving for self-determination, the Russian indictments of "terror" against the Ukrainians lacked the dehumanizing hand of race and racism. Rather, the indictments were countered and quelled by their targets' vivid whiteness. Ukrainians were celebrated as freedom fighters on the basis of their whiteness coupled with Western opposition to the Russian invasion. It took little for Ukrainians, whose faces monopolized the news headlines and timeline feeds, to become universal darlings and irrefutable victims.

The Western world stood alongside President Volodymyr Zelenskyy and the Ukrainians' archetypal whiteness mooted Putin's levied charges of terrorism from Moscow. Ukraine is ninety-nine percent white, and politicians and media outlets all over the world hailed its people fighting for resistance and welcomed those pushed from Ukraine as refugees. As Césaire wrote during the thick of the postcolonial era of the 1950s: "Europe has this capacity for raising up heroic saviors at the most critical moments."[38] This heroism is monopolized by whiteness, embodied decades later by blonde-haired and blue-eyed Ukrainians at the critical moment of NATO expansionism clashing with Russian imperialism.

The war in Ukraine, distinctly unfolding alongside similar campaigns in Muslim-majority contexts, is a powerful theatre illustrating this dissonance. This dissonance frames "nonwhite" Muslims vying for self-determination as terrorists and white Ukrainians, engaged in the very acts of resistance, as freedom fighters. The racial interplay saturates media discourses, scholarly literatures, and as new wars converge with preexisting crusades, across our screens.

We witness it, to the tune of genocide, in Gaza. There an accosted people is slain en masse through the collective indictment of terrorism, holding them unworthy of even the possibility of freedom on account of how they look and how they believe. *One person's freedom fighter is another man's terrorist*, goes the cliché. Yet for some, particularly Arabs and Muslims, the charge of terrorism has extinguished attempts to speak for, let alone fight for, our freedom. "Do you support Hamas?" the question always leveled at the heads of Arabs, Muslims, and Palestinians, on the Piers Morgan show and platforms beyond it, illustrates the latent suspicion of terrorism leveled on our heads, even as our people are accosted by it. Even when and if we answer "yes," our very bodies affirm our guilt.

## Living on Borrowed Time

*Islamophobia and anti-Arab racism are last bastions*
*of acceptable bigotry.*

"This is worse than after the Muslim Ban, than after 9/11," uttered Abed Ayoub, a lawyer and childhood friend, four blocks away from the White House and two decades apart from the day that changed everything.[39] We found ourselves together in Washington, DC, the American capital that engineered the War on Terror and other wars before it, preparing for another crisis that marked our ethnicity and faith as suspicious.

In between the regular combination of doomscrolling and delivering bad news, Abed looked up with a stare that said everything. I had seen that look before. I knew it well. We were, after all, raised in the same two-family home on the outskirts of Detroit, sons of a community that bridged Motown with the Middle East, blue-collar ethic with immigrant grit. We were together years later, no longer children but lawyers and advocates, on the day that then-President Donald Trump signed the "Muslim Ban" executive order one week after his inauguration, setting off the "executive disorder" that would characterize the next four years of our lives.[40]

Abed and I are Arab, Muslim, and American—an amalgam of identities that conjures up "pariah" in the world that we live in. For many who share our identities, or a combination of identities resembling this amalgamation, this is our common reality. But now, it means something different. At this moment, when the horror of mass death unfolds in Gaza and on our mobile screens, our identity exists in absurdity. It spells crisis and contradiction with political happenings near and far.

We see ourselves in the people of Gaza. The accosted people there share our names, our faith, our culture and customs. We have friends in that 140-square-mile open-air prison turned into hell on Earth, including journalist friends who were sheltering at the Al-Ahli Baptist Hospital at the time of the deadly blast on Wednesday, October 18th, an explosion that signaled that this crisis would be drastically unlike those before it.

But what we continue to see on our screens is still half a world away. Until Tuesday, October 17th, when the two distant hemispheres collapsed violently into one. In an instant, the horror of the genocide in Gaza hit close to home.

"A Palestinian boy was killed in Illinois," Abed told me.[41] Unfortunately being American, like six-year-old Wadea Al-Fayoume was, does not protect us from the stigma and therefore the danger of being Palestinian, Arab, Muslim, or from the "Middle East."[42] For far too many Americans and other Westerners, all of these items are callously blurred into one.

Young Wadea was stabbed twenty-six times with a military-style knife. Not by a stranger, but by his family's landlord: a seventy-one-year-old man who's been charged with murder and hate crimes, among other crimes. The attacker also stabbed Wadea's mother more than a dozen times, plunging the knife deep into her body with the same murderous intent. The killer *unsaw* the American status of his targets, and rather, saw the "terrorists" being mowed down mercilessly in Gaza, which granted him license to murder Palestinians standing before him in Illinois.

Unlike her son, the mother *lived*. But what does that word even mean for her anymore?

What does it mean for a mother who escaped war for the safety of an American suburb? What does it mean for Abed and me: an executive director of a civil rights organization and a law professor, standing in the crosshairs of American power with an (Arab) identity conflated with terrorism?

What does "living" mean for millions of Arabs and Muslims who call the United States home, burdened with the impossible task of proving their allegiance, over and over again, in response to bellowing demands that bury our humanity?

What does it mean for students protesting genocide on their college campuses, who are shunned as bigots and shut down violently for decrying what any person of conscience should condemn?

It feels like we are living on borrowed time, like we were extended a contingent form of citizenship that can be stripped at any time, on account of events that unfold in America or on the other side of the world. Our citizenship can be substantively "undone" in whole or in part, determined by the presumptions of terror, and the denied freedoms of speech, assembly, and more.[43]

Calling it "Islamophobia" would be a severe understatement. The existential ballad of being Arab or Muslim in America is far more onerous, far more absurd. It feels like an existence that has *no exit*. An adapted existential play where our daily routine is waking up to the news of war, the stark images and videos of slain children, rolling timelines of shattered villages and the roaring demands "to condemn Hamas."[44] While this plot sounds much like novels from Jean Paul Sartre or Albert Camus, this is not fiction.

*This is our absurd reality.* An absurd reality where we, in America, can only

post on virtual timelines where the heavy boots of suspicion stomp out our voices and censor our speech.

Our names and nationalities, faces and faith brand us with the stain of collective guilt for crimes that we did not commit. Moments like this—like the aftermath of 9/11 or the reckoning after former President Donald Trump's Muslim Ban in 2017—moved many to try to conceal their ethnicity, try to cover their Islam, particularly women who removed their hijabs or young children who hid behind aliases.[45] "Veiling is a political statement," and far more in the era of Islamophobia, an invitation for stigma, scorn, or slaughter.[46] But what was happening during the siege on Gaza seemed more penetrating than in crises before, far more dark and much more daunting.

Hate crimes and incidents skyrocketed after September 11th, 2001, and reached near proportions in the wake of the Muslim Ban. Wadea's death signals that these figures may spike again and descend on the heads of Arab and Muslim Americans shadowed by suspicion. Palestinian or not, since these categories are callously blurred and flattened to mean one and the same thing: *terrorism*. Scholars have spilled considerable ink, and victims of foreign wars even more blood, levying upon Arabs and Muslims this ongoing charge of supporting or sympathizing with terrorists—"Hamas or ISIS"—on account of our names, faiths, and bodies alone.[47]

But we cannot shed our bodies. These are the corporeal vessels that connect us to the victims cast as villains in Gaza. And they are that which bind us to distant places where "wars on terror" were wrought yesterday and are certain to wreck more lives tomorrow.

"Muslims are only newsworthy when villains, never victims." I wrote those words for the first time as a law student weeks after the 9/11 terror attacks.[48] I was much younger then, unprepared for what the world would come to be. But I knew then that it would never be the same.

I typed those very eight words twenty years later in my book, *The New Crusades: Islamophobia and the Global War on Muslims*. In between the wide-eyed optimism of a young law student and the sobered worldview of an aging law professor, 9/11 and today's war serve as bookends for morbid middle passages for Muslims in America and around the globe—as evidenced by the genocidal campaigns in China, persecution in India, hijab and abaya bans in France, and continuing genocide in Gaza. The law and language of Islamophobia have been exported transnationally by an American War on Terror that was first enforced on the home front, upon the heads of Arabs and Muslims like me whose citizenship was cast aside.

Being American was no protection. Not then and definitely not now. The naïve notion that bigotry erodes as time passes was a myth, as the arc of Islamophobia, anti-Arab, and anti-Palestinian hate blurred and blended into an ugly whole as genocide rolled onward.

The barrage of cold stares and commands to condemn terrorism, assignment of collective guilt, and characterization of our dead children as "collateral damage" not only strips us from the substance of citizenship, it renders us

inhuman. "People don't have ideas," wrote Carl Jung. "Ideas have people."[49]

And the idea that conflates our skin with terrorism not only grips the imagination of people but sinks into the very marrow of American gates of power. We must *exist*, whatever that even means anymore, within the very lines that divide our identities and sever us from normalcy.

I am in Washington and not Chicago, but I can feel every one of those twenty-six stabs that plunged into little Wadea's body. And across American cities large and small, *we* see ourselves in the grieving parents forced to bury their dead children in Gaza.

> *This is what it means to be us.*
> *It is time that the world begins to see us.*[50]

What the world would see, in the dark days to come, was the unprecedented onslaught on children. Their limbs would be torn off their growing bodies, and their lives taken before they could grow. The murder of Arab or Muslim and Palestinian children, on the outskirts of American cities and every be-sieged Gazan corner, would be seen by everyone on the screens within their palms.

## Gaza 2.0: The First Digital Genocide

*"The revolution will not be televised,*
*Will not be televised, will not be televised*
*The revolution will be no re-run, brothers*
*The revolution will be live."*
— Gil Scott-Heron

In 1970, following the aftermath of the American Civil Rights Movement, the African American poet Gil Scott-Heron penned words urging people to the streets.[51] The "revolution will not be televised," he echoed, "the revolution will be live." Live inside of public parks and protests on streets of cities like Chicago and Oakland, Los Angeles and my hometown of Detroit.

Heron's timeless words outlasted the Jim Crow reckoning and civil rights struggle that inspired them, and still echo in the minds of the generation that first heard them then and hear them digitally for the first time today. But in that year, 1970, the promise of racial equality was not delivered: the hold of American apartheid remained and morphed into redlining, racial covenants, and new renditions of the old racism.

The movement for Black liberation and existential self-determination, that Heron powerfully echoed, would not be televised. The terrestrial media outlets of the day were rooted in the white supremacy that nurtured racial segregation, leaving the streets as the only outlet for Black protest, and in his words, "revolution."

You had to be there with your body to take part, and march with your feet to be heard.

That was then, and this is now. The world is not what it was in 1970. The advent and emergence of social media has provided new virtual platforms for protest; brave new realms for revolution that force us to revisit Heron's lyrical call to action. These digital venues are vital for aggrieved populations within authoritarian nations, where the possibility of street protests and grassroots revolutions are impossible.

The Arab Spring uprisings are a testament to the "revolution being televised" on social media timelines; flipping the script; and providing fuel for the subsequent phase of assembly, dissidence, and collective protests that unfolded in city squares, streets, and places far beyond and in between. In the beginning, social media platforms "embodied the promise of information capitalism as a liberating and democratic social force that galvanized and delighted second-modernity populations around the world."[52] That promise has been not only broken, but entirely turned on its head as Twitter (now X), TikTok, Instagram, and other social media platforms become digital bastions of suppression and totalitarian control administered by an elite few.

On the other side of revolution are new modes of repression. And on the furthest end of that side, its most horrific iteration—genocide. In this new

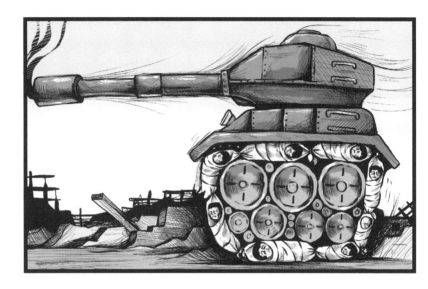

world order, social media platforms have become sites where genocides are enabled and emboldened, scapegoated or justified. And within the lines of those mobile screens that keep us deeply connected, annihilation is vividly depicted for us to absorb on a real-time, rolling basis. Genocides are no longer distant and amorphous phenomena, but passages that we bear witness to as they unfold one victim at a time, one slain human body reduced to a post on a recurring basis. We see, in vivid color, the bodies of children scorched by white phosphorus, and the limp and mangled bodies of civilians laid across fields minutes after a bomb is dropped on a refugee camp.

The inhuman violence in Gaza has pervaded our digital timelines and mobile phone screens more than any other genocide before it. At an unprecedented frequency and with lucidity and transparency, is it a genocide more accessible than any one in human history. We have taken part in this annihilation, and it has taken hold of us. The genocide in Gaza has changed our understanding of what that crime means and looks like, and has *changed many of us* in the process.

Gaza is the world's first digital genocide. A genocide where the images of intimate suffering and death are transmitted instantly onto our screens, seconds or minutes after they have taken place. We see everything, or at least, everything that is captured by witnesses on-site. Witnesses who, in this new age of image and video sharing, who were once ordinary people and are suddenly postmodern-day journalists.

We not only engage with genocide; it absorbs our psyches in the routine acts that have become central parts of how we live today. The gory images of babies with chopped heads are liked and shared, and the streaming videos of children with amputated limbs are passed onto friends and followers with the tap of a finger. Livestreamed footage of bombed hospitals and schools are televised on Instagram Live, while the disastrous shortage of drinking water and food depicted on TikTok reels roll across our phones for individual consumption and mass sharing.

Unlike genocides before, we are immersed in Gaza in ways made by technology that unmake us psychologically. The phones we carry in our palms, an essential part of our daily lives, keep us interlocked between the sights and sounds, visuals and violence of this genocide in ways that are virtually impossible to escape. We are no longer external onlookers. Today our screens keep us more immersed than ever before. This genocide is not distant or foreign to us. We are tracking it on a daily basis and living with it through our screens. It remains front and center on the devices that feed our news and social lives, while feeding us with content that leaves us numb or nihilistic, desensitized to the uncut reel of mass murder and dangerously distant from the feeling of our former selves.

Gaza is hardly the world's first genocide. In fact, there are several concurrent disasters taking place around the world, including in Sudan, Congo, and the dystopian repression of Uyghur Muslims in northwestern China. Yet, the prolific social media traffic dedicated to Gaza and the nonstop avalanche of images, video, and livestreaming shows the how this unhinged violence inflicted on the Palestinian people of Gaza is being absorbed at a historic and

an inhuman rate. The political, spiritual, and historic dimensions of the matter elevate it, but the technology of today has amplified global participation to an astonishing degree. This degree has materially altered how the world sees the Palestinian crisis. Until now, Palestinian victims have long been reduced to faceless blocs of people, or nameless terrorists. Increasingly, that is truly no longer the case, as voices online take to their platforms to memorialize the names, faces, and stories that were not long ago erased from mainstream news coverage, and buried in time.

The genocide in Gaza is not only televised but experienced by all of us in real time. We absorb the uncut violence unleashed upon the Palestinians in a way that no genocide has been experienced before by people not directly involved. For many of us, confined by the events of the genocide despite our best attempts to turn away and move forward, the daily events in Gaza have become our daily events. We are bound, psychologically and existentially to an indelible shock to the conscience and our struggle to make sense of it, of life, and of what it was before. It has become part of us, penetrating our beings.

We must struggle—particularly because of the corporate media's shameful bias—for the truth and transparency that undergirds journalistic ethics. Those ethics are flippantly dismissed by Western media outlets and their corporate handlers, concealing the genuine contours of struggle in Gaza for far too long on television screens and newspaper print. But from an existential angle, these technologies are curating a dangerous new (ab)normal where viewers on all sides are becoming numb to the images of Palestinian death and suffering. Desensitized to a scale of human tragedy that should shake us all; that we should never accept as normal.

These are images that, individually, would not have been printed by major Western newspapers ten to fifteen years ago. Images that should alarm and disturb anyone and everyone. But instead, these visuals of death and destructions are shared and posted, scrolled past casually and passed on to followers and friends with mechanized routine.

Dystopian would be an understatement. This genocide has pushed us to a state far past that, and perhaps, too far gone. If the genocide in Palestine, Gaza 2.0, were a *Black Mirror* episode, we would all be aghast by what the world, and all of us with it, had become.[53] But it is real, and its reel of horrors is more frightening than any television studio could recreate or simulate.

Instead of merely viewing it, we are part of it. We are all witnesses. Virtual voyeurs into a digital genocide that endangers our very humanity with every click and post, share and follow. Instead of observing apocalyptic fiction on wide screens, we are immersed fully in a moribund reality on the roving screen in the palm of our hand. "This is the future. This is the present. This is [hardly]the beginning of big data policing" of pro-Palestinian voices online, but the very apex of it when resistance is more vital than ever.[54] And for those on the ground in Gaza, like Motaz Azaiza or Mansour Shouman, Wael Dahdouh or Bisan Owda, it is a matter of life and death.

This is where all of us are. Trapped. Ensnared in a digital world within a new world order where scrolling past death is a routine part of our absurd new life. The revolution was not televised then, but the telescreens of Gaza have forever revolutionized us from within, where we struggle to make an impact on the people we have grown to love as if they were our friends and family. Because we see their faces and know their names, we come to understand their story, and embrace their struggle as one worth joining. The genocide is televised, and we have all become witnesses.

## An Ode to Anaam

*"Exile is one of the saddest fates."*
— Edward Said[55]

There is exile. And for some, like Anaam, exile that serves as two cruel bookends for a single tragedy.

A fifteen-year-old girl dispossessed from her home and displaced from her village for the first time in 1948 during the creation of the State of Israel, Anaam's childhood was scattered across distant towns like fading memories. Memories and people segregated now by separation walls and bisected plots of nationhood, she was expelled far from the home she knew and the people she loved.

Anaam kept her key, wearing it as the charm on the necklace around her neck, hoping to return to her home one day. She has never returned, and as the push of this genocide foreshadows, she likely never will. The First Nakba, in 1948, led to the making of the modern State of Israel, and the unmaking of Anaam, dispossessed from her home, and the Palestinian people displaced into the wilderness of exile.

That wilderness would claim the state of her life, pushing her from the West Bank into Gaza. Decades passed until the past was once again the present, starting on October 7th, 2024, leading to the raid of her village that pushed her southward toward the Egyptian border. She is ninety now.

Days after the raid, Anaam walked on foot around and across dead bodies and under bombs, scaling four miles, that felt like forever. No longer a young girl, but an old woman. She could not make it alone but had to be held up to make it past the scream of missiles above and the streams of blood underneath.

*The Second Nakba, 2023.* A refugee. All over again.

This time an elder. With deep wrinkles that stretch across her brow like wise branches that reach out from olive trees.

They both have seen too much.

Have cried too much.

Have lived too much.

Have died too much.

Those standing trees and this strong woman, for ninety years and the seventy-five years between twin disasters, two Nakbas, sit atop roots of repeating tragedy, recurring displacement, and perpetual exile.

In Palestine, great disasters happen far more than twice.

For Anaam, this proud woman who resembles our mothers and our grandmothers, there were a million unseen tragedies between the two Nakbas that serve as extreme axes of the cruel tightrope that is Palestinian life.

She is older than the modern State of Israel.

Wiser than any president or prime minister, politician or pundit.

As native as the olive trees that rise from the soil and reach for the sky across the stretches of land she walked over. Once as a girl with olive-skinned innocence, and again as an elderly woman with skin creviced by the cold hands of time and the sun's hot stares. Now an old woman, making that southward trek again with exiled *men in the sun* lifting her up on either side.[56]

She doesn't have to utter a single word. Her image is loud enough. That motley mosaic of tragedies is visible, prominently, on her face.

While the world conspires to erase her name and story, her face renders those attempts fools' quests. These words, which spill from my mind like tears, are my humble vow that I will never forget her face. A venerable face that I saw for the first time on November 9th, and in my mind on each and every day of this genocide since then.

Anaam was far more than one woman. She was an archetype, and even greater, a moving ballad of a people's history of occupation and ethnic cleansing told through two catastrophes, with the fractured chapters of modern Palestinian life in between.

This new story of exile is much like her old one. The new Nakba marching southward in Gaza identical to the past chapter three-quarters of a century earlier. Neither the lapse of time nor the longing for homes changes the face of the calamity of exile, and its shrill finality that shouts down the inner voice lying to its victims about an imminent return home. In his stunning autobiography, *I Saw Ramallah*, Mourid Barghouti writes,

> In the disaster of 1948 the refugees found shelter in neighboring countries as a "temporary" measure. They left their food cooking on stoves, thinking to return in a few hours. They scattered in tents and camps of zin and tin "temporarily." The commandos took arms and fought from Amman "temporarily," then from Beirut "temporarily," and they moved to Tunis and Damascus "temporarily." We drew up interim programs for liberation "temporarily x" and they told us they had accepted the Oslo Agreements "temporarily," and so on, and so on. Each one said to himself and to others "until things become clearer".[57]

The passing of time and the reality of unfamiliar surroundings, for Palestinian exiles, made chillingly clear that a return home would not come. Exile was permanent, even when life was temporary.

These words are an attempt to give Anaam a modicum of justice that the world perpetually denies her and all Palestinians in Gaza and beyond, to memorialize an individual whom the pen of imperial history conspires to keep faceless and nameless, buried underneath the pages of texts that unmade the truth and the peoples that cling desperately onto it.

This is an elegy to forgotten faces who died during that trek into the wilderness of exile, killed once by bullets and again by the imperial hands of historians. An ode to exiles of today, roving toward the "safe zones" of Rafah that are instantly turned into killing fields, moving waywardly from place to place, between life and death, until the realms of geography and existence blur into an amorphous whole.

Like Anaam, who survived both Nakbas. I see you and all your pain. I just wish my words were half as strong as your will. I wish my words could move across the stretch of time like your feet were cruelly forced to roam, to grant you rest and relief.

Anaam brings to memory the brilliant Palestinian novel, *Wild Thorns*, and that peculiar pain of exile in motion captured in its pages. The author, Sahar Khalifeh, wrote, "Sink into the mud, oh Palestine of mine, and let the seaweed cover you! Let's say goodbye homeland and finish with it."[58] That purgatory of exile drives you toward madness, toward the seduction of giving up on the dream of return and giving into the nightmare of leaving for good.

The wild thorns of exile pick and poke at you long after the trial's physical eviction. They, like torture, push you to surrender and keep going, and going, and going, until you never look back and you bid that final goodbye. That is the design of those who impose exile. That is the aim of ethnic cleansing.

But then you look at faces stronger than yours—faces like Anaam's—and witness the roots of archetypes and olive trees—olive trees that whisper so quietly: people die, but exiles end. Individuals transition onward, but ideas take hold in the very places that spawned them.

For good. And, for *good*.

## Don't Call it a Ceasefire

There have been no ceasefires for forty-seven days and seventy-five years.

Only moratoriums.

Only *humanitarian pauses*.

Only *conflict pauses*.

Only existential flux trapped inside an open fortress.

These phrases, all of them, are political devices deployed to save face and temporarily conceal the genuine face of genocide.

Those who peddle them, particularly American politicians or Western news pundits, should be brave enough to be honest and call it a diplomatic smoke screen for mass killing.

Call it a Trojan Horse for the delayed bombing to come.

Call it any one of these. But don't call it a ceasefire.

On Wednesday, November 22nd, 2024—nearly seven weeks into the genocide—word began to spread that a "ceasefire" was on the horizon in Gaza. These two words, among the orbiting calls of "genocide" and "ethnic cleansing," rang from protests and social media posts, were strung across headlines and expressed from heads of state condemning the Israeli military's disproportionate siege on Gaza.

For forty-seven consecutive days, the Israeli military has bombarded the people of Gaza with craven disregard for human life. They have dropped dumb bombs and shot munitions indiscriminately, exposing that mass killing was part of their military design. As the statistics rise toward genocide and the destruction spirals toward disaster, the numbers of dead Palestinians and decimated infrastructure cannot begin to tell the story of the endless ballad of bloodshed that has monopolized life there, and for many of us, wherever we stand.

Among the bloodiest days has been the day before the "ceasefire." Particularly during the hours before its enforcement. On Friday morning, as minutes ticked off before the pause on bombing, the Israeli military has accelerated its offensive, bombing homes and refugee camps, destroying the Abu Hussein school operated by the United Nations, and massacring displaced refugees exiled from their villages and towns.

The death toll has skyrocketed during those liminal hours. As bombs have dropped and bodies fell along with them for that final time, the Israeli military has unleashed unimaginable furor on civilians. It is as if their military aim is to maximize the opportunity to kill before the window closed; to push forward the project of ethnic cleansing before the clock strikes *stop* . . . for now. This is the storm before the "ceasefire," the deceptive phrase peddled by state enablers and their corporate media interlocutors that know better, but still sell hope to people on the ground in Gaza whose lives hang in the balance of each line and lie.

Reality, however, confirms that it is anything but. A ceasefire denotes

permanence, *finality*, an end to violence. Not contingency, transience, or as the hundreds more killed on Thursday and Friday morning before its imposition have embodied, a green light to murder as many Palestinians as possible before the clock ticks pause.

A "ceasefire," mainstream media outlets dub it. But the enhanced violence that has unfolded in the precedent hours and minutes before the pause revealed that it is anything but. That it will bring, following its four-day scope, no cessation, stoppage, or slowing of genocidal militarism.

Rather, this opportunistic barrage unveils that Netanyahu and his enablers, most notably Joe Biden, are invested in the very opposite. This "conflict pause" is two things: first, an opportunity to free the Israeli hostages; and second, a marketing campaign to sell the image that Netanyahu's government is "humane" and "civilized" to a global community. A community that has closely observed its boundless barbarism, and in turn, witnessed the inhumanity that Palestinians in Gaza have faced for decades. But in reality we can all see that in the darkest hue of collective punishment and apocalyptic rage, this is no ceasefire.

Calling it such obscures the genuine objective behind this conflict pause, both Israel's open violation of the humanitarian pause before it, and the augmented genocidal violence that will surely come on the other side of it.

What then is the overall aim? It is ethnic cleansing. A process that is neither paused nor stopped during this four-day stretch, when more than a million Palestinians pushed from northern Gaza remain trapped between homelessness and being pushed even further south. When 900,000 displaced Palestinians from the central and southern corridors of Gaza move between bombed buildings and shuttered hospitals, with the only pathway for medical care across the border in Sinai.

A circumstance, even if a genuine ceasefire is had, that will conclude with every single Palestinian in Gaza having to come face to face with the sobering reality that their homeland has been irreparably destroyed and is utterly uninhabitable. A circumstance in which choosing to remain—among the remains of memories past and dead bodies present—risks their health, the well-being of their children, and their very lives as a mounting Israeli occupation bent on annexation rolls in.

Netanyahu and his government want to make that option, of *remaining in Gaza*, impossible for its native Palestinian population. That is the aim of this pause and every inch of this military campaign surrounding it.

This is no ceasefire.

Again, there have been no ceasefires for forty-seven days and seventy-five years. Only the voracious violence of a government committed to eating up as much land as possible, and a global appetite for Palestinian death that seemingly knows no bounds. Putting a stop to that appetite for Palestinian death, permanently and without the language or lies of pauses, is the only genuine ceasefire that can be had.

# Part II

For Reem & Hind

## The Next Sinister Stage of Ethnic Cleansing

*"[C]olonization works to decivilize the colonizer, to brutalize him in the true sense of the word, to degrade him, to awaken him to buried instincts, to covetousness, violence, race hatred, and moral relativism."*

— Aimé Césaire, *Discourse on Colonialism*

For fifty days, the Israeli military has pummeled Gaza with unrelenting violence. The world stands idle, permitting one of world's most sophisticated armies to collectively punish one of its most vulnerable populations. Other nations, like the United States, have enabled this genocide as full-fledged co-conspirators and financiers, backing the onslaught at every turn while peddling vain rhetoric about ceasefires and humanitarian concerns.

If shooting crabs in a bucket was a military project, Gaza would be it.

The rising death toll, underestimated at 13,000, testifies to that bleak analogy. Images of apocalyptic destruction, spanning the north of Gaza to the besieged central and southern corridors, form a panorama of dystopia that spells genocide in one of the most densely populated plots of land in the world.  The militarized genocide in Gaza creates the landscape for its sinister companion: ethnic cleansing.

Ethnic cleansing, in lay terms, is a project whereby a government uses force or intimidation to expel an ethnic group from a territory, to make way for another ethnic group. Ethnic cleansing is forcible mass displacement, and in Gaza this strategy has been deliberately preceded by a menacing architecture of explicit and conspicuous violence that climaxed horrifically during these past fifty days.

While the terms are often used interchangeably, *genocide* and *ethnic cleansing* overlap but are teleologically distinct. *Genocide* fixates centrally on the *people* as subjects of elimination, while *ethnic cleansing* focuses mainly on the *land*. Within the ethnic cleansing calculus, the people are collateral objects to be expelled and eliminated, and the land is the central subject of concern. It is the priority, the site of intellectual and physical focus, to be occupied, annexed, and then remade for another people—in this instance, Israeli settlers.

Since October 7th, this aim of ethnic cleansing has exploded onto the heads of the 2.3 million Palestinian residents of Gaza. It has taken the form of incessant bombing, stealth grounds invasions, and the disconnection of water, food supplies, and Internet to a people besieged, ignored, and even more, flatly vilified as "terrorists."[59] This militarized front of the broader ethnic cleansing campaign destroyed mosques and schools, bakeries and homes, critical infrastructure, and possibly most horrifyingly, hospitals.

Hospitals: the very sites where tens of thousands of dying and injured Palestinians flocked for lifesaving care have become the principal targets of military violence, most vividly portrayed at the Al the Shifa Hospital. Ground zero for the "medical ethnic cleansing" program in Gaza, Israel clumsily scapegoated Al Shifa as the site of Hamas's Command Center, and then brutally transformed the site meant to save lives into a mortuary for mass death.

The lowest point came on November 18th, when Israeli soldiers occupied the hospital, then forced hundreds of physicians, staff, and patients to walk out at gunpoint, waving white flags while rolling off in wheelchairs and hospital beds.

This seemed to be the plan all along. Destroying hospitals, and the medical infrastructure at large, was a central component of Israel's ethnic cleansing program. While hellbent on taking as many lives as possible with missiles, bombs, and indiscriminate shelling, the more clandestine strategy of shuttering hospitals and shattering the medical landscape offered a more ominous, more effective ethnic cleansing strategy.

Palestinians fleeing closed hospitals, and the newly injured, needed treatment. With nowhere to go for medical treatment, hundreds of thousands of Palestinians in Gaza in need of vital medical attention would have to leave this land entirely bereft of functional hospitals. They would have to migrate, *en masse*, from a native soil barren of water, fuel, and physicians toward a southern border where makeshift hospitals awaited them.

Far from home, across a border that would transform them from indigenous residents into stateless refugees. Once, and very likely, for good.

This mass exodus is accelerated by the bleakest version of "medical apartheid," accomplished with the making of hospitals into mass killing sites.[60] This is part of Netanyahu's strategy: bombing hospital after hospital, and systematically destroying every branch of a Gazan medical network that was already on unsteady legs before this crisis began.

However, this unfolding plot of medical ethnic cleansing is hardly the most sinister part of the broader Israeli military program. Its next phase, which is already being peddled by the Netanyahu regime, reflects its most diabolical twist.

Last week, both Netanyahu and his finance minister, Bezalel Smotrich,

began pushing "voluntary migration" of Palestinian refugees from Gaza as the "right humanitarian solution."

The messaging spin here is as depraved as it is deceptive. Above all, there is nothing "voluntary" about migration here. Palestinians in Gaza and beyond want nothing more than to stay in their land. However, Israel has emaciated the Strip of anything and everything that makes it inhabitable for its residents. And most urgently, destroyed the very hospitals that enable them to remain alive.

Therefore, this migration and mass exodus is not only *involuntary*, but the direct consequence of the genocidal violence Israel inflicts on Gaza and its network of hospitals. There is nothing "voluntary" about it and framing it as such further exposes a regime so far gone from international law and the truth that it is mind-boggling.

Next, Israel pins the responsibility of absorbing the masses of Palestinians refugees in Gaza in urgent need of humanitarian aid on Arab and Western nations. Smotrich stated: "The reception of [Palestinian] refugees by the countries of the world that really want their best interests, with the support and generous financial assistance of the international community and within the State of Israel, is the only solution that will bring to an end the suffering and pain of Jews and Arabs alike."[61] In sinister political speak, Smotrich placed the burden on the international community to not only take in the waves of displaced Palestinians from Gaza, but also pay for their relocation and acclimation to exile.

This was the plan all along. To bomb with open disregard for human life; decimate infrastructure against the accord of international human rights law; emaciate the land from food, fuel, and water; blackout the residents from access to Internet and the rest of the world; descend and then destroy the hospitals vitally needed to treat limitless waves of injured, ill, and dying Palestinians; and finally, make the land so insufferable, so uninhabitable, that Palestinians clenching onto their land with whatever they have left have *no choice* but to leave.

Netanyahu has annihilated Gaza and pushed Palestinians out of their homes and off their land, so that he can rebuild it for Israelis only. However, the exile that awaits scores of Palestinians beyond Gaza has been unfolding for decades. The current languishing of Palestinians within disconnected lands across the West Bank, Gaza, refugee camps in the Middle East, and the global Palestinian diaspora manifests the exile and fracture of a people striving for a state. Palestinian novelist Sahar Khalifeh speaks of the experience of exile among those in Gaza, writing, "Exile: a reality we experience in the heart of the motherland itself."[62]

Regardless of how Israel spins it, there is nothing "voluntary" or "humanitarian" about this next phase of ethnic cleansing. The United States and the Western nations who are enabling this ethnic cleansing will flank alongside Israel and their diabolical reframing of reality, but much of the world sees through it. And sees it and its allies parading as "civilized" as pariah states in the making.

## The Soul of My Soul

*"I kissed her, but she wouldn't wake up."*[63]

Reem, only three years old, was the apple of Khaled's eye. More than a loving granddaughter, Reem was his loyal companion. She would mimic him as he made his daily prayers, climb atop his lap when he drank his morning coffee, and peer at him from the window of their Deir al-Balah home when he left for his afternoon walk.[64] She was *jiddo* Khaled's diminutive shadow, following his every footstep until she found herself back home in his arms.[65]

The siege traumatized young Reem. But her grandfather would hold her during intense periods of bombing. The crash of airstrikes and the panorama of death encircled her young body. And her late-night cries had become part of the apocalyptic soundtrack of genocide in Khaled's Gaza home.

The cries came to an abrupt stop one early morning on November 28th, 2023.[66] Khaled was not home as Reem slept in her final resting place. Israeli airstrikes on the neighboring Al-Nuseirat Refugee Camp struck their home, taking the young girl's life.[67]

Khaled walked home and noticed a glaring void in the window. He finally saw Reem when he arrived, but was met with a limp body instead of a vibrant little girl rushing toward him with extended arms and a wider smile. He lifted her up in front of cameras as he kissed her little forehead. "She was the soul of my soul," the grandfather cried, holding Reem with the very hand that welcomed her into the world.[68] It is a cruel world for children in Gaza, slain too soon by no fault of their own.

*"The soul of my soul."*[69] The world absorbed the weight of those five words, far heavier than the body of little Reem. However, they say that the smallest bodies have the heaviest coffins, a phrase that affirms that the weight during times of war is measured more by emotional toll than physical pressure. The social media world memorialized those words, "the soul of my soul," with digital posts and reels, memorials and viral messages. Khaled's pain was evident for the world to see, as were the lines and crevices on his face as he mourned his slain granddaughter.

Khaled was shattered but calm, engulfed by the sorrow of a grandfather who just lost his granddaughter. He did not promise vengeance, shout battle cries, cite scripture, or show anger as cameras locked in on him. Global audiences saw a mourning elderly Palestinian man, dressed in the traditional Islamic *thobe*, donning a beard, and keffiyeh around his head as a victim. Yes, *a victim* of aggression that claimed the life of his granddaughter. Not a terrorist, which the world has long associated with his clothes, customs, and complexion. Terror came crashing down on him, he was its victim, not its purveyor, social media posts affirmed and echoed.

"I kissed her, but she wouldn't wake up." Khaled uttered into the cam-

eras, which prompted a video gone viral. Those unscripted words would become a rallying cry, a slogan etched upon protest banners and emblazoned across shirts.[70] "She was the soul of my soul," he repeated, staring into Reem's face a final time before handing her off to a stranger tasked with finding her final burial spot. Khaled would never hold her again.

Memories of Reem were buried six feet deep. Deep, under the rubble of their shattered home. Deeper into that week, Khaled found one of her dolls in the rubble. While speaking to CNN, he held it in his arms like he once did Reem. Then, he lifted the doll's face to meet his own and kissed it on the forehead. "I used to kiss her on her cheeks, on her nose and she would giggle," Khaled said, gripping the lifeless doll, remembering the soul he lost.[71]

Khaled would become a new kind of Palestinian archetype, a different sort of symbol for men reduced to terrorists and caricatured as emotionless. His every word showed otherwise. Around the world, viewers witnessed a vignette of a Palestinian elder, whom old media outlets had only counted as a faceless statistic or an unseen figure in a monolithic crowd of suspects. But

Khaled's story, echoing the meaning of his name, retold the "eternal" tragedy of a grandparent mourning the death of a grandchild. The story told, for the first time with meticulous detail, in the unseen colors and masculine contours of life in Gaza.

Sensitive and vulnerable, pious and resolute, soft and loving. The world marveled at Khaled's dignity and strength, and his surrender to Islam as a source of solace. It was the very faith of the legions of Gazan men and women who lined up around destroyed mosques for Friday prayers and holidays during the siege.[72] Portraits of Islam that old media outlets overlooked and ignored, much like they did when it came to reporting on the hundreds of mosques destroyed during the siege. This was the Islam that Khaled embodied for the world to see, and, after that viral video of him kissing Reem's forehead, for the *world to love*. Khaled was no extremist or zealot: he was just a grieving grandfather.

A man who *lost his soul* to a criminal siege. A soul in which the world discovered a sublime version of Muslim masculinity. A sole shadow existing between the subaltern and sublime shadows of Gaza, who rose from its unseen corners to mourn his beloved granddaughter, Reem, whose name and face we will always remember because we cannot forget Khaled's words.

## What About the Men?

*"These babies, these ladies, these old people are bombed
and killed.
So, we urge Israel to stop."*
— Emmanuel Macron, President of France[73]

*"The world is watching, on TV, on social media . . . witnessing
this killing of women, of children, of babies. This has to stop."*
— Justin Trudeau, Prime Minister of Canada[77]

The boys and men were lined up like criminals.[74] Even worse than criminals, they were treated like "terrorists." Blindfolded and handcuffed. Stripped naked from head to toe.[75] Everything torn from their brown skin and scarred limbs. Except for the underwear and narrow strip of cloth around their eyes.

No names. No faces. No backstories or front-facing vignettes. None of that mattered. They were a herd not to be heard from or seen extracted from history and humanity all at once.

Their individuality entirely removed by marching orders that flattened the mass with the gavel of guilt. *That* cardinal stain and counterterror sin, of *terrorism*, enabled the soldiers to do whatever they pleased with them. The terrorist, after all, is the most hated figure in the modern world, who deserves whatever punishment is doled out against him. His very existence is reviled, and very sight repulsive to all who value anything civilized and sacred.

*"Yalla, yalla!"* The men and boys walked under the order of soldiers and over the barrels of guns. They walked, and walked, and walked, until they reached a nameless patch of brown soil.

Then stopped, suddenly, when shouts rang out. Sensing that death could come at any moment, they peered into the pitch-black of darkness or death, which blurred into a single vision during the siege in Gaza.

*"To your knees!"* a soldier shouted, in familiar Arabic accented by a foreign tongue. He repeated, "to your knees!" until every bended Palestinian knee touched the dirt. Dirt their fathers and grandfathers and forefathers tilled and toiled atop, now the site for the most morbid passages of their family histories.

The captives, from boys in their early teens to elders approaching a twilight that may never come, dropped to the ground. Gaza is no country for old men, the picture affirmed, and one of those rare places on earth where innocence is foreign to youth.

This, however, was their home. A place forever turned around and upside down by sights no human brain should absorb. A plot that no man or boy, woman or girl should have to experience firsthand. Yet, that is precisely where they were, laid and lined across an expanse of dirt they once walked past on the way to work, kicked a football across to a friend, or raced by after a trip to meet the warm faces and the embrace of loved ones at home.

Their eyes opened and faced forward. Then lowered, with their heads prostrate and their bare bodies lined neatly in a morbid ritual that resembled the holy prayer that the Holy Land knew so well.

But it was not Friday and was no prayer.[76] Not Jewish or Christian, Islamic or otherwise. The soldiers lording above the men confirmed it. These Palestinian men and boys were dropped to their lowest limits, shoulder-to-shoulder, reduced to sheep for slaughter. Prey, not prayer. Masculine subjects of scorn instantly indicted of "terrorism" by War on Terror law and logic endorsing that presumption, one which violently penetrated Gaza with a limitless rage after October 7th, 2023.[77] Only God could save them.

What crime or sin ushered them toward this hell? These boys and men were students, doctors, academics, and journalists.[78] They were civilians. Not soldiers or terrorists. Again, none of that mattered *then and now* and in between mass airstrikes and more massacres. Under the guise of "counterterrorism" and the "shared rage" of propaganda, the details of who they were as individuals were flattened violently to create an indistinguishable line of terror suspects.[79]

Exclusively male suspects. Men and boys, whose race, religion, and *gender* were strung together to form the indictment. That pointedly Arab, Muslim, and masculine indictment that reemerged, violently, after September 11th terror attacks that unfolded on the opposite side of the world, coordinated by predominantly Saudi culprits disconnected entirely from Palestine and Gaza.

But the world saw them, Arab and Muslim and Middle Eastern men, as one caricature. This construction was less an outcome of "intersectionality" but rooted in the Orientalist and Islamophobic discourses seared onto their skin.[80] Scars of guilt inflicted upon them shortly after they were born, which spread more prominently across their bodies as they aged from boys to men. Scars that mark them as symbols of terrorism, singling them out for collective arrest, humiliation, and slaughter in Gaza.

*"Get up!"* The boys and men were ordered back onto their feet. Denied food and drained of energy, the young among them made it to their feet while the elders staggered and struggled. Some fell, then limped back up to avoid falling for the final time. Then, they were carted off like sheep in cargo boxes of Jeeps, herded by soldiers who snapped photos of their bare bodies with mobile phones. Then minutes later, posted their images across social media for the world to see. "Human animals," after all, is what Israeli leaders called the men of Gaza.[81]

The pictures went viral.[82] *Instantly.*

Virality, as new age propaganda, was their aim. To publicize the dominant narrative that "terrorists were captured," which would justify expansion of the siege into Gaza under color of law or the War on Terror's black hole of illegality.[83] Two months after the horror of October 7th in Israel, the siege spirals into scenes that resemble the dystopian miniseries, *Black Mirror.*[84] But they are real, and the *chill* of it all reveals that this is no Netflix miniseries. Rather, it is another dark episode where Orwellian propaganda travels at light

speed, faster than the genuine identity of the men underneath blindfolds and the truth behind their alleged "terror ties."[85]

But neither truth delayed, or due process denied, matters. Not for these men and boys. "Two plus two equaled five," plus seven men shot and killed on site that day in Gaza.[86] It all amounts to "socially constructed," theater of "captured terrorists." Civilians stripped of their plainclothes who had commited no crime and done no wrong, but even so they were dressed in the modern costume of terrorism endorsed and enabled by law, propaganda, and the dominant racialization of Arab and Muslim men.

These slain men and boys are a cautionary tale that "War on Terror" law and discourse renders lives fair game for mass indictment and arrest, extrajudicial torture and slaughter. Perhaps more men found that very end of indignity in between the barrel of the gun and the black hole of detention. While those who are still breathing endure a double captivity that locks their bodies behind the bars of presumptive terrorism while being captive within the "open air prison" of Gaza.[87] Confined inside of Gaza, and then collectively slain by a genocidal fury rooted in manmade fiat that casts Arab and Muslim men as indefensible enemies. The War on Terror, and its barrage of laws, lies, and lines of terrorism trope manufacturing, came crashing down violently on the men and boys of Gaza.

———————

When Edward Said wrote, "I am an Oriental writing back at the Orientalists, who forever thrived upon our silence," he did so as a Palestinian scholar.[88] But even more narrowly, he penned that perspective from the vantage point of a Palestinian *man* in a world where his gender, combined with his ethnicity, signaled a distinct meaning. A distinct kind of threat.

Said's landmark work, *Orientalism*, was a text about the systematic European and then American demonization of the "Muslim world." The distortive epistemology he dismantled was deeply gendered, even if not explicitly, with analysis rebutting the orientation of Arab and Muslim men as the principal purveyors of fundamentalism, violence, and warmongering.

Said, a Palestinian man and exile, surveyed the world from that lens. While the world saw him and his Arab and Muslim male counterparts as security and demographic *threats* and reported as such on corporate media outlets and newspapers, Western governments conspired by enacting laws that policed, punished, and prosecuted them. This was true before the terror attacks of 9/11, and prolifically the new world order following them.

Gender remained central to the demonization before and after that cataclysmic event. While Arab women were caricatured as submissive and suppressed, and Western feminist efforts to "liberate them" rhetorically beat the drums for war within *progressive* spaces, the men were always the primary targets of violence.[89] This was "liberalism in service to empire," as stated by Deepa Kumar, packaged with the rhetoric of progress to advance ethnic cleansing.[90] Men, and boys nefariously aged into men, remained the principal objects reduced into "human animals" whose only reason for being was terrorism, then systematically killed because of that ascription.[91]

The terrorism caricature is pointedly masculine. Arab and Muslim men are instantly guilty, stripped of the presumption of innocence and the right to due process. They are never individuals, judged on the merits of their actions or distinct idiosyncrasies. Rather, Arab and Muslim (boys) and men are overwhelmingly lumped into an anonymous monolith; their bodies inspected and interrogated through the lens of terrorism that instantly brands them with the presumption of guilt.

They are terrorists until proven otherwise.[92] And that *until* seldom even comes. This, after all, was how the war crimes in Iraq were permitted to roll forward. And indeed, how the genocide in Gaza was sanctioned after the events of October 7th. Men are branded with that damning indictment of terrorism by a system of Islamophobia that is rooted in the Orientalism Edward Said reckoned with four decades ago; which rises back to the fore in the rhetoric of Netanyahu, Ben Gvir, and Smotrich.[93]

We saw it, most virulently, on December 7th, 2024, in Beit Lahia in the northern section of the Gaza Strip. On top of bombed soil in between shattered homes and shuttered businesses, Palestinian men were laid down like criminals, stripped of their clothes and their dignity, then lined into rows.

They were civilians. Men who worked at schools and shops, government agencies and banks. Many of them were fathers, all of them sons, who lost loved ones during two months of genocidal violence that seemingly has no end. They, too, were victims.

The particular and individualizing facts of who these men are, like their clothes, were violently stripped from view. In an instant, the world saw them through the lens of terrorism. And the Israeli military capitalized on the immense imaginative pull of this stereotype ascribed to Arab bodies to claim that they were "Hamas fighters." Whether they were or were not, in the public imagination and so many Western media outlets, did not matter. What matters is that they are Arab men, Palestinian men, only seen by so much of the world through the prism of terrorism. Which is to say, not *seen* at all.

Their faces and names, ethnicity and geographic locale provided the cor-

poreal evidence needed to draw that conclusion, and the Israeli military weaponized that stereotype to claim a staged military victory. Then, the Israeli
Defense Force (IDF) peddled the propaganda for all the world to see. They
would see it in the image of beaten down, bare naked Palestinian men lined
across their native soil, then dragged off like cattle toward a destination that
ended with torture, death, or some morbid stop in between them.

The world gave them the green light. Principally, the United States, War
on Terror machine, which for decades now has given global license to the trope
that Arab and Muslim men are presumptive terrorists unless proven otherwise.

It's a trope echoed by pundits and politicians during what has so far been
a sixty-day stretch, even among those calling for a permanent ceasefire. Canada's Prime Minister Justin Trudeau, five weeks into the onslaught, stated that
Israel must stop "this killing of women, children, babies" in Gaza.

*He made no mention of Palestinian men.* Four days earlier, President Emmanuel Macron of France stated:

> *These babies, these ladies, these old people are bombed and killed. So, there is no
> reason for that and no legitimacy. So, we do urge Israel to stop.*

Palestinian men, again, were conspicuously absent from his words. Entirely absent, as individuals worth saving, from Macron's call for a ceasefire.

Palestinian men, in Macron's words and in so much of the world, are nonexistent as real human beings, let alone victims. They are putative terrorists unworthy of being seen through the humanizing lens of individuality. And therefore, unworthy of being saved from the march of genocide that marks them as terrorists, wherever and whoever they are. The demonization of Palestinian men is a project rooted in longstanding Orientalist narratives and emergent Islamophobic discourses. Their humanity is written out of news stories and redacted from demands for ceasefires.

Intentionally, by design, because prevailing interests are invested wholly in the demonization of Palestinian men, and the destruction of a masculinity conflated with terrorism. This is why innocent men are paraded around as terrorists, stripped of their dignity and stripped of their masculinity, for the whole world to see. Humiliated, then reduced to animals and objects of scorn.

We saw it in Abu Ghraib, and we see it, again, in Gaza.[94]

That is how the world has come to see us.

I see myself in those men. My faith and name, phenotype and ancestry connect me to them as I peer at their sullen faces and bare bodies from a screen.

A screen where the only guilt I see is worn by their captors, and the complicit and conspiring governments that enable this inhumanity.

---

**Day 64**

## Meta vs. Palestine

The erasure of Palestinian voices is not only unfolding in Gaza. The project to silence and suppress them, and their allies, is also taking place online.

On Instagram, especially, citizen journalism and advocacy pushing for balanced coverage has been met with a relentless system of censorship. In the midst of siege, netizens took to their phones to display and discuss the events in Gaza, where speech and assembly erupted digitally. Instagram was the site of this sublime transnational rebellion, which traversed nations and cultures to form the most formidable global movement standing for Gaza. Across its digital pages and stories, where the battle to make Palestinian suffering seen and its vanquished voices heard, Meta has pushed a nefarious front of corporate authoritarianism. A front that shares the same aim of the military siege of Gaza—to remove and "thin" out Palestine from its digital landscape as well as its physical landscape.

Sixty-four days into the crisis, we can see the myriad ways Instagram—and its mother company Meta—silences content about Palestine. Many of us have been targeted and directly affected.

Accounts are flagged, features are disabled, we lose the ability to like or comment on a post, and/or restrictions are placed that limit our posts from being seen beyond our existing following. Removed posts, flagged accounts, and the widely feared suspended account, the modes of suppression seem limitless, and are anchored by the mysterious shadow-ban that confines the reach and visibility of targeted users. The objective goes beyond mere censorship, but is, in the words of Ruha Benjamin, "born from the goal of . . . social control."[95]

All of these modes of punitive censorship and control, levied upon those on the ground in Gaza or in nations far from it who expose the genocidal violence being inflicted on its people, have skyrocketed. Despite Instagram's claim that it never "intends to suppress a particular point of view or community," the past two months tell an entirely different story. These grueling days have affirmed that Instagram carries out a clandestine policy of suppressing pro-Palestinian voices.

This is far more than a speech moderation problem, or a biased algorithm at play. Instagram is invested in concealing the horror in Gaza, as well as silencing Palestine and the swelling legions of voices galvanizing around its besieged people. The motives appear to be many, including an institutional pro-Israel positionality rooted in economic interests, professional binds, and most saliently for the purposes of this essay, strategic partnerships with Israeli government bodies.

Instagram's "algorithms of oppression," to quote Safiya Noble, that directly or disproportionately censor pro-Palestinian accounts have been widely examined.[96] As are the unequally enforced community guidelines around "harassment" and "hate speech," which incentivize pro-Israel users

to report content conveying the carnage in Gaza or showing solidarity with its victims. Pro-Palestinian voices are being punished for merely typing or saying the words "Gaza" or "genocide," and are digitally bullied by pro-Israeli accounts weaponizing Instagram's community guidelines to suppress speech.

But this is just the tip of the iceberg of the digital architecture of suppression Instagram imposes on voices advocating for Palestine. And it has far more than a mere chilling effect. What lies beneath the surface is more ominous, and debunks Instagram and its mother company, Meta's, claim that it is *objective and neutral*. Rather, "the math-powered applications powering [Instagram are] based on choices made by fallible human beings," alumni of Israeli government agencies or executives with ongoing ties.[97]

Instagram maintains a robust and ongoing relationship with several Israeli government agencies. In fact, it has a strategic partnership with the Israeli Cyber Unit—an extension of the Israeli Defense Force (IDF). The Israeli Cyber Unit, also known as Unit 8200, "is an Israeli Intelligence Corps unit of the Israel Defense Forces responsible for clandestine operation, collecting

signal intelligence (SIGINT) and code decryption, counterintelligence, cyberwarfare, military intelligence, and surveillance."[98] Through direct and ongoing collaboration, Instagram shares user data and content with the Israeli Cyber Unit; responds to requests to tailor its algorithm in line with elevating favorable content and against oppositional content; amplifies military propaganda; and tracks the online advocacy of targeted accounts that are flagged as "disruptive."

Those who are seen as *disruptive*—or online activists—are punished in the myriad forms described above, from disabled account features to suspended accounts. This mode of digital suppression that counts the IDF as a partner illustrates why Instagram is wholly positioned against the voices in, and for, Gaza.

It exposes why *Meta vs Palestine* is far more than just a pithy title, but an online reality. A dystopian reality unfolding in online terrain where the very military that bombs and bludgeons innocents in Gaza is similarly hellbent on erasing Palestine online. But the strategic and structural ties between

Instagram and Israel are more expansive than the IDF's Cyber Unit. Instagram has direct ties and maintains ongoing communication with the Israeli National Prosecutor Office. As of December 1st, this Office has issued 9,500 requests to Instagram to remove pro-Palestinian content.

Of these requests, 95% have been accepted. A staggering figure, which since December 1st, has likely risen in terms of frequency of petitions and acceptance rate. Conspiring with the genocide on the ground in Gaza, Instagram has systematically worked to cleanse its digital terrain of Palestine and those who advocate on behalf of it. Instead of arms and tanks, the weapons of mass cyber-suppression are algorithms and shadowy ties to the Israeli military.

As ethnic cleansing unfolds on the ground in Gaza, the erasure of pro-Palestinian voices parallels it online, signifying another frontier of repression and resistance that has pulled us all into war. A digital front where speech is censored, suppressed, silenced, and slain.

## No Christmas in Gaza

During the third month of genocide, Christmas will be celebrated by 2.4 billion people, globally. And yet, Christianity as a whole in Gaza faces elimination. That phrase sounds like embellishment, or alarmism. But the numbers of remaining Christians reveal it to be soberingly true. And yet there is no mass outcry from Christian communities worldwide.

*'Tis the season* when pine trees are adorned with presents and ornaments, while downtown corridors in cities near and far are illuminated with the lights and sights of Christmas. Everywhere *except* the birthplace of Christianity. Today, in the heart of the Holy Land, the native sites of ethnic cleansing speak volumes about the hypocrisy of Western nativity scenes. There is no Christmas revelry, this year, in Gaza. There are no silent nights. Just an

endless string of unholy nights of bombing and bloodshed.

As I pen these words in Washington, DC, where the wrapping of the holiday season is sublime and ubiquitous, Christians in Gaza are facing extinction. Only 800 – 1000 Palestinian Christians remained in the Gaza Strip *before* the genocide. A staggering figure, made even more striking by the statistic that puts the entire population of the besieged territory at 2.3 million.[99]

Gaza, particularly its Zeitoun neighborhood, *was once* a thriving center of Christian life. Only 120 miles away from Nazareth, the boyhood home of Jesus, and the formative holy sites that pull Christians from all over the world in pilgrimage, it is an absurd reality that Christianity faces complete erasure in Gaza today.

But this is precisely where this genocide has brought us, today, less than a week before Christmas. Despite this harrowing reality, there is little "outcry" from Western Christian communities, no alarm from evangelicals or urgency from conservative American politicians. They all, despite their fellow Christians facing elimination, are silent as the onslaught ensues unabated.

This is a silent erasure within a broader genocide. An unseen ethnic cleansing within an ethnic cleansing where churches and community centers, Christian homes and Christian life, are being wiped out of Gaza.

"This community is under threat of extinction," shared Mitri Raheb, an Evangelical Lutheran pastor from Bethlehem. "I'm not sure if they will survive the Israeli bombing, and if they survive, I think many of them will want to emigrate."[100]

On November 10th, 2023, roughly one month into the genocide, *Al Jazeera English* estimated that only 800 Christians remained in Gaza. Across the faith's array of denominations, more than a month later, with the aggregate death count conservatively estimated at 20,000, one can assume that many of the people killed were Christians.[101]

But the grim reality of genocide in Gaza quickly does away with the need to assume anything. On Sunday, December 17th, a mother and daughter were shot and killed in front of Holy Family Catholic Church in Gaza.

The cold-blooded murders were captured on video, at the doorstep of the beseiged church where hundreds of Palestinian Christians remained trapped inside.

Confined within a church, without food and access to the outside world, "fearing to get shot," many of these people will be among those added to a death toll skyrocketing by the day. My longtime friend, Fifi S., has family inside of that church.[102] We spoke, against the bars of censorship via Instagram only minutes after those two Christian victims were killed, about her family. Her parents, family members, and friends were among the hundreds of Christian captives holding onto life and holding onto the existence of an entire faith group, inside of that church.

"These people, my family and my friends, have not been able to leave the church for eight to nine weeks," Fifi revealed. "Their homes have been demolished, and this is where the Christian community felt they would be safe."

Sadly, they were wrong. The Israeli military has violated virtually every human rights standard during this crisis, including the blatant attack on Muslim and Christian houses of worship. On October 19th, 2024, the neighboring Church of Saint Porphyrius was bombed, killing at least eighteen people.

"500 people are inside of that church," shared Fifi. What was thought to be a safe haven for Gaza's Christian community has become a killing field.

The vast majority of remaining Christians in Gaza are, currently, stuck inside of that very church. 500 out of a total 700 Palestinian Christians still living in Gaza are trapped within a historic house of worship that has become another site of an unholy genocide. A place and people that the world has ignored. Erased from the same mainstream media coverage and headlines, and digital media pages and timelines, people who celebrate the holidays that originate on their soil.

"We all know that within this generation, Christianity will cease to exist in Gaza," shared Pastor Raheb.[103]

In these coming days, the sounds and sights of Christmas will be all around the world. The glee of children opening presents and worshippers

congregated in churches will be seen both online and in homes, and across city squares, streets, and parks. But not for Palestinian Christians in Gaza. They are trapped within a church and a land that may be their final resting place. And what may be the final site of existence for a people, and an entire faith group in Gaza, facing the threat of permanent erasure.

This year, and every year onward until the ethnic cleansing is stopped, *there will be no Christmas in Gaza.*

## Motaz, Our Brother from Gaza

*"I know what the world has done to my brother and how narrowly he has survived it."*
— James Baldwin, *The Fire Next Time*[104]

*"We still alive. Till now."*
— Motaz Azaiza[105]

He walked atop a hill of rubble, piled up between destroyed buildings and darkness. The dust of death filled the air, with its black and grey hues swallowing every shade of life that once colored that corner of Deir al-Balah.

But no more. The Gaza of yesterday was buried underneath the rolling apocalypse of today. "The past was dead; the future was unimaginable."[106]

Everything was black and grey. Except his bright blue vest and bloodred teddy bear, which Motaz lifted into the lens of the camera.[107] A camera tethered to a phone that would be his mouthpiece to the world. His brown eyes stared up in that direction, sitting beneath eye glasses and atop a black beard that, in Gaza, signals masculine terrorism. He understood the shade of that indictment too well.

*What deprives the spirit of its colors? What is it other than the bullets of the invaders that have hit the body.[108]*

Motaz, his lean and tall body affirmed, was a man. And a Gazan man at that. His name means "proud" in Arabic, a word he modeled and inspired so indelibly in the days of siege that spiraled into months of genocide. The line between life and death blurred into one as Netanyahu crossed red lines, as men and boys were crossed out of existence.

He lifted the red bear up into the pink-and-white sky, proclaiming that he was still alive. That "we" are still alive.[109] The red bear was no white flag, but rather, a banner of protest. A symbol of innocence.

Survival in Gaza, in and of itself, was an act of resistance for any man or boy. Motaz held the bear up atop the very soil where he buried tens of family members only days before.[110] The bear, juxtaposed with his bearded face and brown skin, rebutted what presidents and prime ministers uttered, what War on Terror laws enshrined, and what media narratives trumpeted about brown men made into black shadows.

Yellow journalism faded in favor of the real-time blues of boys and men in Gaza, like Motaz. His five-word statement formed an elaborate liberation theology. A subaltern counter-narrative that reclaimed Palestinians from foreign hands and distant laws that made them into monsters. Motaz did not mention "men" or "boys." Not explicitly at least. But the gendered tenor of his words radiated rebelliously from his skin, as the masculine blues and blood reds beaming from it affirmed who he was speaking to, and about.

He was asserting his manhood before the world. More specifically, his Arab, Muslim, and *Palestinian* manhood, rooted in that narrow strip of land that he once roamed as a boy, and that raised him into a man. The Gaza he knew was gone. The youthful innocence of the twenty-four-year-old was now buried underneath the debris and dead bodies he walked atop.

But he was still alive. The world watched him through dystopian screens and digital windows that we carry, faithfully, in our palms. Windows into a counter-narrative of resistance, *masculine* resistance, from a man who breathed life into us day and night, we peered into that black mirror to see Gaza through the eyes of Motaz.[111]

The young, bearded Palestinian emerged onto our timelines from the rubble of Gaza. He was compassionate and committed, resilient, and most importantly, unabashedly human. The vast majority of us, on Day 1 of the siege of Gaza, did not know the name "Motaz Azaiza." 107 days later, when Motaz evacuated Gaza for the safe haven of Qatar, that name is one that we will never forget.

Motaz was far more than a citizen-journalist or a survivor. He was, and is, a walking embodiment of how the world finally came to know Palestinian identity in all of its layered complexity, plight, and fight.

He allowed us to see his pain, intimate and immediate, firsthand. The loss of fifteen family members at the onset of the genocide, clad in the blue vest with the word "press" tattooed across it. A marker that we thought put him among the few that Israeli bombs or bullets could not touch, but which proved mythic as the days of genocide violently mounted and claimed the lives of over 120 of his journalistic colleagues.

We saw his unwavering dedication to his land and his people, every day. Day in, day out. Carrying a camera that looked outward into the besieged strip and inward into his eyes, fusing his indigenous soil with the contours of his visage. As the days progressed, the two blended into a singular whole.

Motaz, for billions around the world, *became* Gaza. The land and the lad blurred into one, which humanized both for a global audience that only saw war and violence, terrorism and tyranny in anything and *everything* Palestinian, whether in human or geographic form.

We saw Motaz carrying bloody-faced babies who he did not know into the cabin of a car racing toward or away from another bomb site.

We saw Motaz hoist up a red teddy bear atop an apocalyptic canvas of grey, with his feet rooted in a land that he did not leave during the thick of the genocide.

We saw Motaz document the mass exodus of Palestinians toward the southern border, a modern Trail of Tears textured by the intimacy of real faces, and real people.

We saw Motaz. He allowed—invited—us to see him. And by seeing him, we grew to know and love him as if he was our own family member. The Palestinian brother whose daily episodes in war-torn Gaza would quickly become our own. Geographically distant perhaps, but so proximate and close

to our hearts and minds as we absorbed the stark images and footage from behind the black screen.

We saw Motaz. Scrolling through his stories and page during both the day and the night, and those liminal spaces in between.

We prayed for Motaz, fearing the worst, during those silent passages in time when we did not hear from him. Those stretches when he did not post an update, a story, or a tweet, fearing the worst for our new brother from Gaza. Hoping, and holding our breath, that he was not among the night's victims.

We saw Motaz. And in him, we saw something far more transformative and transcendent than any one individual. For many of us, particularly in the West, we saw a complex Palestinian man who shattered the prevailing stereotypes that pervade CNN and the BBC, Fox News and corporate media outlets that discursively flatten an entire people into terrorists.[112]

We saw a living and vivid model of Palestinian, Arab, and Muslim masculinity that dismantled those damning stereotypes ascribed to our men and boys. "Warmongering and violent," they say, "lacking emotion" and brooding, indicting us before the world truly knows who we are.

We saw in Motaz the very opposite. During the 108 days, the young man's soft voice and unyielding dedication to capturing what those news outlets buried, revolutionized our conception of Arab and Muslim masculinity. It was a rolling case study against Orientalism and Islamophobia, in real time, where a living protagonist embodied the layers of manhood—from levity to love, softness to sadness—seldom applied to our old men and young boys, fathers and sons.

We saw this in Motaz. Our brother Motaz.

We saw him age, rapidly, over those bloody 107 days.

We saw bullets race by his head, nearly grazing the face we grew to know so well and love even more.

We saw his perspective sink into gloom and anger, as the genocide extended in time and expanded in scale, stealing the innocence of youth and the will to live.

Finally, we saw ourselves in Motaz.

The very best of who we aspired to be, during a time of genocide when the excesses of Western life spoil our spirit and bury our gratitude.

Motaz forced us to see ourselves, then look beyond the limits of our daily routines and first world problems; to see Gaza as a place worth defending, and Palestinians as a people who demand our action.

We saw a friend and brother in Motaz, whom we grew to love so dearly because of his sheer commitment to his land and his people.

We also saw a mirror of aspiration in Motaz, a young man whose whole life has been enveloped by occupation, open-air prisons, and then genocide, a walking tale of courage and fearlessness that we hope is buried within us all.

Motaz, on January 22nd, evacuated Gaza. But the imprint he left within billions around the world will remain lodged deep in the native soil of our souls. While evacuating, he never really left Gaza. Not in spirit, as he tirelessly travels the world testifying to the horrors of genocide. His departure was bittersweet. While rooted in Gaza, he showed us what media outlets conspired to conceal for far too long: the suffering of a people, the suffering of his people.

But his brushes with death were close. Far too close, and too frequent. Motaz was still young, despite grey hairs and grim trauma leveled on his head by genocide. *If only the world celebrated survivors who unveiled hard truths as much as it does fallen martyrs.*

Motaz lifted himself from the rubble, one final time, to live onward. The most memorable heroes are those who rise from the lowest rungs of anonymity and despair to shake the world in their direction, against the indomitable tide of media conglomerates and imperial presidents.

Motaz not only survived the genocide but authored a subaltern narrative of Palestinian humanity and complexity, courage and strength that will always stand.

For that, brother Motaz, we are forever indebted to you.

## Aaron Bushnell
## and the Rage Within

*"After all, in the final analysis, man is a cause."*
— Ghassan Kanafani, *Palestine's Children*[113]

I'm still shaken.

Twenty-four hours after watching the video, the young man's face as he paced stays with me. The words he uttered while he stepped toward the site of his final protest echo loudly in my head.

"I am an active-duty member of the United States Air Force, and I will no longer be complicit in this genocide."[114]

He spoke, looking away and toward the camera, as he took steps closer and closer.

The pain on his face signaled more than fear. Aaron, after all, was only twenty-five. The reality of what he was about to do was sinking in, deeper and deeper, while the weight of genocide compounded by the creep of suicide dropped hard on his shoulders.

You can see it on his face. You can hear it seep from his voice.

> *I am about to engage in an extreme act of protest. But compared to what people have been experiencing in Palestine at the hands of their colonizers, it is not extreme it all.*[115]

He marched forward, like a soldier. That was, after all, who he was. Who he signed up to be. Forward, on the margins of the Israeli Embassy on International Drive in Northwest Washington, DC—at the intersection of the two principal culprits of this genocide.

Israel and America. The flags of the two nations waved behind him as he placed his military cap on his head. Bushnell was not merely an American, but an American soldier. He wore that badge on his chest. Proudly. The stain of guilt from "complicity in genocide" inflected his voice and infected his camouflaged uniform.

Unlike most Americans, Bushnell understood his nation's central role in Gaza's rolling demise. The reality of 40,000 slain Palestinians burned him with guilt and buoyed him to undo his military service in radical fashion. There would be no honorable nor dishonorable discharge for Bushnell. He would take the matter into his own two hands. One hand carrying a camera, and the other a canister of gas. The episodes of pain and uncertainty, fear and commitment that reeled forward as Bushnell stepped toward his final stage were just as painful to watch as his last act.

For me, they were even more painful.

I'm still shaken. I can still hear those words and see his face.

The video, from beginning to end, is something I will never unsee. A

"FREE Palestine"

Aaron Bushnell

young man struggling with guilt and grief, desperation and rage, driven to do the unthinkable until it was unthinkable no more.

Only twenty-five years old. The premeditated protest felt like a bleak, existential play for a new genocidal chapter in human history. The nihilism spawned by the moment birthed a radical form of protest for Bushnell, much like the extreme powerlessness that moved Mohammed Bouazizi to do the same more than a decade ago in Tunisia.[116]

To quote Sartre, there was *no exit* for Bushnell. Except the one he believed to be most impactful, and most memorable. And he was committed to taking it.

Before he doused himself with gas and lit his body aflame, a voice inside my own head spoke to me. It whispered, "*I wish I could have reached Aaron.* He looks like one of my students, who could have engaged in protest in ways that did not involve harming himself, that did not require him to take his own life."

"Maybe he shared one of my posts, read one of my books, or followed me on social media," I reflected. "Maybe I could have persuaded him to not do what he did, what the whole word would see on their mobile phone screens."

But, perhaps, that was his intent. His final act of protest would also be his final day in this world, on this earth.

I am sorry that the world, that Gaza, that genocide, that your nation and my nation drove a young man to kill himself in one of the most horrific ways that somebody can kill themselves.

Unlike those acts of suicide performed in solitude, Bushnell's act was intended for the world to see. His suicide intimately wed to genocide, performed before the world's collective eyes for the sake of others, for the sake of Palestinians in Gaza, desperately moving to shake everybody toward action—toward action that, no matter how strong, could not match the courage of his radical act.

Bushnell proceeded to set his body ablaze. Then the flames raced across his arms and legs, torso and head, eating the skin from the face we saw minutes ago. A face that will always be part of this moment in world history, central to this genocide, the face of a man who had never set foot in Gaza.

The flames slowly ravaged his young body and burned the very life from inside of it.

*He would never be the same.*

*I will never be the same.*

We were undone, forever. From what we saw on February 25th in front of the Israeli Embassy; and from what we and he saw from October 7th, 2023, through this very day. Until his final day.

The lines between sanity and insanity blur dangerously for all of us. Maybe we're all crazy. The lines between reality and absurdity have never been so tenuous. Those lines are dissolving by the constant reel of death that invades our timelines and infects our brains, designed to numb us to the uncut evil of unrestrained genocide.

Bushnell was no cautionary tale, and his final act was not deviant or aberrant in substance. He represented something within all of us as we are gripped by the weight of this genocide and gripped by the chill of its horror.

He represented our struggle with the reality of the scale of slaughter that shook us, and the brutal truth that no degree of Arab death will stop the marching orders of genocide.

I will remember Bushnell as an everyman, not an exception. A real human being instead of an inhuman spectacle, who shouted the very two words that we all utter on our chosen stages of protest.

*"Free Palestine!"*

Bushnell's stage was different, and that familiar phrase were his final words. The rage and pain that burns within all of us burned outside of him, eating him alive until he was no more.

Until he was no longer a man, but a symbol.

A symbol that will stand vividly in our minds and burn in our hearts. For good, and *for good.*

## Man on Fire

*I wrote this piece shortly after the death of Aaron Bushnell, who took his life as an act of protest in from of the Israeli Embassy in Washington, DC on February 25th, 2024. I performed it for the first time at an event for Gaza in Toronto, Canada, three days later.*

Meet me at the intersection of the Israeli embassy
And American empire.
Draped in camouflage green that can't camouflage
What burns in between my white skin
and the dilemma I'm in.

I enlisted as a wide-eyed teen but didn't sign up for this.
Brown children with charred skin
Little kids without limbs,
Flour massacres and famine
Old women and new Nakbas
Roll across my mind's eye and timelines
As I scroll past my sanity
Toward a page between nihilism and despair.
Guilt and despair,
Anger and despair,
Rage and despair,
Complicity and despair,
Solidarity and sadness,
Masculinity and madness
Burning everywhere inside with no place to hide.
Meet me at the intersection of the Israeli embassy

And American empire.
Staring inside my soul as I speak into this camera.
With a canister of gas in hand ready to make my final stand.
My mind won't rest 'til this last protest.
I know you see me.
You will see me now or see me later.
Atop that digital plaza, home to the rubble and ruin of Gaza.
Do you see the veiled fear in my face?
The lost innocence in my grin,
The vain strength of my chin.


Please don't romanticize my valor or virtue.
I'm no hero.
Unlike Motaz, Wael, or Bisan,
I'm a just a simple man.
Just like everyman and everywoman.
A man who's tired.
A man on fire.
Every hour, on fire.
Every day, on fire.
Every night, on fire.
I can't put it out.
Mind, heart, and soul ablaze
By countless dead bodies over 140 days
Of military homicide,
Made-in-America genocide,
That endless stalk of suicide,
From this black mirror it rises . . .
Violently from my very palms into the center of my eyes.
I see it, around the clock, when asleep and aware,
Death and despair,

Drones and despair,
Famine and despair,
Rolling across this screen and ripping out everything between.

There is "No Exit," in the words of Jean Paul Sartre,
Just nameless Arabs slain across Gaza beaches, at each day's start.
For 140 days and 140 nights.
But this Sunday, this Bloody Sunday, is my final fight.

Meet me at the intersection of the Israeli embassy
and American empire.
I've seen it all,
Every hue of hubris
Every shade of *shirk* and color of contradiction.
Underneath every Biden or Bibi quote
Are white lies at most,

Black women lifting up red hands for vetoes,
With fingers doused in blood like Cheetos,
Trotted out by diversity, inclusion, and empire
Pimping black bodies on postmodern auction blocks,
Uniting nations divesting aid like corporate stocks.
"Civilized?"
I don't see that in Netanyahu or America,
But it radiates from the soul of South Africa,
You see that whiteness that enslaved and maimed,
Manifest Destiny, rape, and claimed
The supremacy of the white underneath the camo I'm in.
Conceals a vile terror unmasked.
White skin and black masks,
White lies and bleak facts,

Of enabling genocide,
Funding and financing genocide.
This is no country for old men,
Except the sleepy one at the helm.

This camouflage can't camouflage that history,
Or the sinister passages of mystery,
Of fires next time and this time,
Lit in the name of the wonder of whiteness,
Dubbed sublime and supreme,
Supreme and sublime,
And every virtue inside
The founding fathers of laws that buried native truths,
    daughters, and sons.
Proud sons.
Indigenous daughters.
Black mothers.
Palestinian fathers.
Their faces burn within and across this white skin I'm in.

Meet me at the intersection of the Israeli embassy
and American empire.
Where I will prove to you.
All of you.
Each and every one of you.
That I am more than this white skin,
Far more than the army fatigues and the tired lies stitched across them.
This is my last stand.
An American soldier's last stand.
In front of American and Israeli flags waving behind,
But the colors of Gaza draped 'cross my mind.

An Air Force cap atop my head,
An invisible keffiyeh wrapped round my neck.
My right hand making that final salutation . . .
While the left starts my-self-immolation.

I'm afraid.
Those images of slain children cut across memories of my
    own childhood,
The laughter of friends I will never hear again,
The touch of a love I will never know again,
And the embrace of my mother I will never feel again.
Never. Feel. Again.

Now, I just feel and smell gas,
Cowardice and gas
Complicity and gas
Cravenness and gas
Genocide and gas,
Suicide and gas.
Lit aflame by this rage within that explodes across inches of this skin.
This elevated skin of mine,
Which laws hold out as superior, supreme, divine,
Unlike these kids in Palestine,
Whose lives don't mean an ounce of mine
That you hold up as sanctified
Peels off this skin like clementines,
Just like those kids in Palestine.
Their skin burns off like that of mine.

They rise and fall, burn and die for a Free Palestine.
A Free Palestine.

Burning from my lips
Burning from my limbs
Burning from these hymns.

*"But this extreme act of protest is nothing compared to what
children in Gaza must endure."*

Bodies fall but ideas endure.
Bodies burn but ideas endure.
Empires fall but ideas endure.
Empires burn but ideas endure.

# Part III

For Aaron & Issam

## A Ramadan Starved By Genocide

For the vast majority of Muslims outside of Gaza, fasting for Ramadan is a spiritual mandate. For those trapped within its bloody walls, fasting is a deadly imposition this Holy Month.

While 1.8 billion Muslims around the world will be fasting, 2.3 million Palestinians in Gaza will be starving. Or, at minimum, sixty-five percent of that population standing at the intersection of ethnic cleansing, famine, and Ramadan will face hunger as a matter of genocidal design, not religious conviction.

One hundred percent of Palestinians in Gaza face a heightened degree of food insecurity, with sixty percent gripped by full-fledged famine. Famine is worst in the north of Gaza, as articulated by Palestinian activist Zeena Aqeel, "where 300,000 people are barely clenching onto life amid grey rubble and rumbling stomachs."

This is Ramadan in Gaza.

A season of starvation crossed with genocide, colored by the apocalyptic strokes of shattered mosques and the ongoing strikes of Israeli jets.

While Muslims globally will begin the traditional annual fast on Sunday, March 10th, 2024, a mounting number of Palestinians in Khan Younis, Rafah, and emaciated Gazan villages beyond and in between began *fasting* well before that date. These fasts were not Islamic, but wholly sacrilege, inflicted by an Israeli war machine that plotted a famine as part of its broader ethnic cleansing project.

It did so in a series of sinister steps, or unholy pillars of a starve and slay campaign that began on October 8th and continue into the Holy Month of Ramadan.

The first was to destroy bakeries and centers of food production. By strategically destroying these spaces, Israel aborted Gaza's capacity to create its own food supply from within. This made Gaza, and its millions of besieged residents, entirely reliant on external aid, and dependent on donations from the outside world.

Next, Israel wielded total control over Gaza's water supply. Starvation was exacerbated by denying access to clean water, which Israel turned up by turning off two to three of the water pipelines that pump drinking water into the Strip.[117] With no clean water coming in, desperate Gazans turned to contaminated sources to drink, cook, and clean themselves during the thick of the genocide. This not only fueled the deliberate famine campaign, but also killed children and adults denied water, the very lifeline of life.

Third, and perhaps the most nefarious to date, Israel conspired with the United States to stigmatize the United Nations and Reliefs Works Association (UNRWA)—the primary organization tasked with providing emergency aid to Gaza.[118] It did so, strategically, after the International Court of Justice (ICJ) rendered its "historic decision" on January 26th, as an attempt to dis-

tract global attention from the ruling.[119] By tying UNRWA to terrorism, the principal pipeline for food provision was not only cut off, but legally criminalized. This was unprecedented, given UNRWA's attachment to the UN and Western roots. Yet, it marked a central and sinister plot to convince foreign governments to divest billions of emergency aid funding to Gaza, and turn starvation into widespread famine across a strip of land that had become a food desert. Linking UNRWA to terrorism enabled Israel to bomb their buildings and food stockpiles within the Strip, resulting in the destruction of 155 installations via airstrikes and ground attacks.

The criminalization of UNRWA also enabled the next and fourth step of its genocidal famine campaign: Israel's complete border closure to foreign aid. By conflating UNRWA with Hamas, and thus, terrorism, Netanyahu ratcheted up the starvation project by restricting the entry of all foreign aid into Israel. Whether from charitable sources, churches and mosques, governments, or humanitarian groups, foreign food aid was denied entry by sea, land, and air. As a result, stockpiles of food spoiled as it waited on the other

side of Gaza's borders, while within it, legions of starving people were being weakened as bombs fell from the sky and famine rose from the ground.

Fifth, and circling back to Ramadan, the Netanyahu regime is conscious that its famine campaign will bleed into the Holy Month. In fact, Israel bombs Gaza virtually every year during Ramadan as if it were some diabolical tradition, desecrating Ramadan for Palestinians and also for Muslims globally. This year is far more pernicious, with at least 144 mosques flattened and razed inside of Gaza.[120] By destroying almost every center of Islamic life in Gaza, the Israeli regime sought to emaciate the spiritual lives of Muslims in Gaza as it starved their bodies of food and water.

This was their plan. But as the proverb goes—man plans, and Allah laughs.

The opposite took place. In a sublime stroke of faith, Palestinians prayed alongside and inside destroyed mosques, convening in unprecedented numbers—*while starving*—to pray on Friday services across the Strip.

The images were as stunning as they were inspiring, foreshadowing that the genocidal conspiracy to starve Gaza physically would not eat into them spiritually.

This brings us to Ramadan, when the genocide will intrude upon the Holy Month, and remind us that our fasts are not like the fasts of the people in Gaza.

Our fasts will end with bountiful tables of food, water, and more importantly, safety.

Gaza's fasts began with no food, will end with scarce crumbs, and remain encircled by genocide.

"We fast because we have no food," shared Mohammed, a friend on Instagram, "and will fast on Ramadan because we will have no food still."

During these thirty days of Ramadan, let us always be conscious of the rolling 155 days of genocide in Gaza, and push our bodies and minds to do everything we can to alleviate the starvation and struggle of our people in Gaza.

## Disintegration

*"I leave you with photographs, pictures of trickery, stains on
the carpet, and stains on the scenery."*
— The Cure, "Disintegration"[121]

These beheaded babies needed no verification.

The charred and headless bodies, dangling from the arms of a man
shouting into the camera, affirmed what had unfolded only minutes before.[122]

Before the viral video raced across digital platforms and claimed a permanent plot in our mind, Rafah became the site of one of this genocide's
most gruesome massacres.

A massacre not measured by scale of death or degree of destruction, but measures far more sinister. Incidents that we saw in naked, living color, projected onto the screens of our mobile phones that these days double as mortuaries.

Morbid black mirrors where headless Palestinian babies hang from the blooded hands of refugees, camped behind humanitarian centers reduced to death camps.[123]

Sunday, May 26th, 2024, will forever be remembered as the "Rafah Tent Massacre." I gave it that title hours afterward online. And it became known that way to many of the subaltern voices so often closed off from the process of writing history. Our mandate is to etch into words gory images forever etched into our minds.

These images of beheaded babies could clearly be seen and verified by age and name, face and family. This is in contrast to those supposed forty beheaded Israeli babies that were touted by those politicians hellbent on genocide, and media headlines beating the drums of a siege that would decimate a people and their plot of land. Of those babies, there was no video evidence. Just hearsay. No names or ages of the alleged babies were produced. Merely rhetoric from American presidents and an Israeli prime minister primed for genocide.

Without verification, the myth of beheaded Israeli babies was echoed by Joe Biden and the corporate media architecture conspiring with the plot to destroy Gaza. The degree of journalistic malfeasance cannot be overstated, as leading newspapers printed and peddled the lie without checking sources.

However, as Nazi propagandist Joseph Goebbels stated, "If you tell a lie big enough and keep repeating it, people will eventually come to believe it." Particularly those already in invested in the decimation of the Palestinian people, and others sitting on the imperial fence of journalism where corporate media outlets dominate the dissemination of information.

The march of genocide rolled over the lie and those bent on exposing it, as Israel and the United States trampled the rule of law, journalistic ethics, as well as a global community that incessantly called for ceasefire at the United

Nations and the halt of genocidal acts at the highest courts.

There were no beheaded Israeli babies. But it did not matter.

The lie had been weaponized and widely disseminated, and the myth morphed into a genocidal vendetta that displaced millions and murdered thousands. It conjured up in the halls of American and Israeli power to—once again—indiscriminately punish the "uncivilized" and repay the "savages" locked away in an open-air prison camp of their making. The view of "Arabs as savages" was hardly a new one for Netanyahu, but one passed on from within his very household before he rose to the highest rungs of state power in Israel and unleashed the siege following October the 7th.[124]

In between the lie and the last massacre, evidence of beheaded babies was finally produced. It sprung from our screens, so vividly violent, that we could not turn away if we tried.

A baby. Or what was once a baby. His head severed from his little body by a 2,000-pound bomb made in America, held by a man as evidence —inhuman evidence—for the entire world to see.

Verification. Finally.

Fact, not fiction, burned in the minds and hearts of millions shook by an image that signaled yet another turning point.

Another flour massacre.

Another Al Shifa siege.

Another uncovered mass grave.

Another Aaron Bushnell.

Another Hind Rajab.

Another smoking gun.

Another body of evidence that signals that this genocide has descended into something far more sinister, spiraling into a depth far more hell than earth.

The truth is right there, hanging headless before our eyes.

But sadly, on a landscape ravaged by unchecked Israeli militarism and unhinged American might, the blatant lie of headless Israeli children means everything, while the truth of beheaded Palestinian children means nothing.

We must face this imperial word by memorializing the events of genocide from our perspective, then beheading it with the swing of our pens that bleed dignity into the headless bodies of babies and hope into the hearts of those who cannot unsee them.

We see these dead babies in the children living there, here, and in our hearts.

> *"To kids in Gaza my vow right now,*
> *I'ma ride for your life like you were my child."*
> — Macklemore, "Hind's Hall 2"[125]

## Machine Dreams, Digital Nightmares

*"Each person has his darkness.*
*Each person has his right to darkness."*
— Mourid Barghouti, *I Saw Ramallah*[126]

*"We shall meet in the place where there is no darkness."*
— George Orwell, *1984*[127]

"I try to sleep—I cannot sleep. I write a fragment here and a fragment there. Casual observations, summaries of a conversation. When I switch off the light and close my eyes the sounds of my life start rising in this quiet, dark room. Thoughts and questions and images from the life that is past and the life that awaits me, awaits us."[128]

In the same way that Ramallah haunts Palestinian writer Mourid Barghouti, the images from Gaza—the digital pictures of the mothers wailing while holding dead newborns in shite sheets; images of fathers digging their black nails into brown soil in search of children dismembered by bombs; pictures of elderly women with wrinkled brows, wearing the wages of genocide and displacement in their faces as they limp southward toward new Nakbas and repeated exile; scenes of rows of naked men, who look like me, lined up like cattle across their native blocks and neighborhoods, these things have opened my eyes to the point where I cannot close them. I can never close them again.

Not even during the thick of night and its din of darkness. When sleep creeps in, to usher me toward that other side where the temporary escapism of rest or the reel of nightmares awaits. It sometimes comes. Other times, it does not. My phone, always close by, looms more menacingly than the grim reaper and the sandman. It pulsates, shines, and shakes these days, to remind me of another atrocity, another airstrike, another massacre, another blown-up school or blown-up mosque, another boy who will never become a man because his name found itself on a kill list fed to an AI-driven program called "Lavender" that decides who lives and who dies.[129]

*"I never sleep, 'cause sleep is the cousin of death,"* Nas rapped on his classic album *Illmatic*, echoing a Gaza "state of mind" held by billions around the world who saw the women, children, and men as more than just digital matter.[130] Saw them as human beings—all of them—real people who matter.

This is not the case in Gaza. Perhaps it had not been for decades, according to the dominant War on Terror narrative that made men into monsters, and boys into terror suspects. But even these old discourses are making way for new, far more sinister directives. Directives of kill lists and threat scores that reduce Palestinian men and boys to data, and pursue them with new age killing machines that massacre with spectacular efficiency and without feeling. The dominant new currency is data, where software engineers feed the old, gendered War on Terror stereotypes and anti-Palestinian tropes into inputs that form new genocidal algorithms. The killing machines, given clever names like "The Gospel" and "Lavender," can rapidly process massive amounts of collected data on the entire population of Gaza to identify who to kill by targeting, and who would die as collateral damage.

The sheer scale of death in Gaza is unprecedented, largely, because of the "dangerous new precedents" of AI killing programs and machines.[131] These technologies are able to target, destroy, and murder at scales far more efficiently than approaches controlled wholly by humans. Apart from being the "most asymmetrical war ever," as one Israeli law professor called the siege, the events in Gaza mark a new moment in (in)human warfare.[132] A war of machines against man, high-tech innovation powered by algorithms deployed against women, men, and children who were previously and historically not seen as legitimate human beings, now seen even less so by reducing them to data.

The darkness of Gaza is now digital. Two AI-driven machines have been central in the mass destruction and mass killing in Gaza. "The Gospel" is an algorithmic program used to target buildings, while "Lavender" is processed by lists of names — the overwhelming majority of them men — that are set out for slaughter.[133] Both of these programs order soldiers operating tanks, drones, fighter jets, and more to pursue the building or person ordered by AI. Thus, machines are now issuing military orders to soldiers, expediting the process of who can be killed and "accelerating the 'kill chain' to increase" the number of victims.[134] Journalist Sigal Samuel explains,

> *"Gospel" marks buildings that it says Hamas militants are using. "Lavender," which is trained on data about known militants, then trawls through surveillance data about almost everyone in Gaza—from photos to phone contacts—to rate each person's likelihood of being a militant. And "Where's Daddy?" tracks these targets and tells the army when they're in their family homes . . . because it is easier to bomb them there than in a protected military building.[135]*

The kill lists, and targets, are overwhelmingly men. This lines up with how "terrorists" and "militants" are defined and then identified by the IDF, again rooted in the gendered War on Terror discourse that singles out men as monsters. Thus, the algorithm inputs are deeply gendered and in turn, create algorithmic outputs that conflate terrorism with masculinity. The same old dominant messaging with new age packaging, illustrating Noble's thesis in *Algorithms of Oppression* that racism and gendered biases are "baked into" the inputs of the AI systems that control search engines and kill during sieges.[136]

*Algorithms of genocide*, one may call "The Gospel," "Lavender," and the other systems the IDF has deployed in Gaza to usher in a new passage of dystopian darkness. Israeli leadership denies the use of such programs, but whistleblowing from IDF soldiers and a report by *+972 Magazine* published in April tells another story. The report was a scathing indictment, revealing how AI has "played a central role in the unprecedented bombing of Palestinians, especially during the early stages of the war."[137] The findings rely heavily on the testimony of six Israeli intelligence officers, who revealed how the IDF gave "sweeping approval" for IDF officers to "adopt, 'Lavender's' kill lists."[138] Again, the military hierarchy was one where the machine kill lists issued the orders, and the "human personnel often served only as a 'rubber stamp' for the machine's decisions" to bomb family homes, residential areas, and a milieu of other sites across Gaza.[139]

Again, the vast majority of names on the kill lists are Palestinian men. Men who are broadly classified as "terrorists" and often tenuously linked to Hamas, are assigned a threat score computed from a range of innocuous data including age, religion, telephone activity, family name, and more. In short, being a man or boy in Gaza, alone, would elevate one's threat score to a number that would place an innocent civilian high on the list. Again, the algorithms used by "Lavender" are deeply gendered, with the masculine indictment of terrorism a central input.

However, the targeting of masculine terrorists was used to justify the collective punishment of the people in Gaza and the mass destruction of the land. Pursuing terrorists was the War on Terror scapegoat for the sinister objective of decimation, dispossession and displacement. The Israeli intelligence whistleblowers affirmed this,

> *In an unprecedented move, according to two of the sources, the army also decided during the first weeks of the war that, for every Hamas operative that "Lavender" marked, it was permissible to kill up to 15 or 20 civilians; in the past, the military did not authorize any 'collateral damage' during assassinations of low-ranking militants. The sources added that, in the event that the target was a senior Hamas official with the rank of battalion or brigade commander, the army on several occasions authorized the killing of more than 100 civilians in the assassination of a single commander.*[140]

By removing the decision-making authority of who to kill, and who can be killed, from military men to machines you also shift culpability. The scale of "collateral" death, most women and children, is a predictable margin of error ("mistakes were treated statistically") assigned to the function of the AI killing machine, not the military general or lieutenant.[141] Machines make errors, but cannot be brought to trial like men or women, ushering in a new regime of war that enables scales of killing that evades legal redress and invades uncharted bounds of logic.

Within the Panopticon of Gaza, everybody's information is accessible and every action recordable. The AI machine gives "every single person in Gaza a rating from 1 to 100, expressing how likely it is that they are militant."[142]   Again, the men and boys overwhelmingly comprise the top of the lists with high threat scores, whose homes are targeted and bodies stalked. The cases of Wael Al-Dahdouh and Motaz Azaiza, whose family home was destroyed by airstrike and who was steadily stalked by drones until forced to leave Gaza, respectively, provide popular case studies for how threat scores shape targeted assassination attempts.[143]

As a strategy to save money and maximize killing, the IDF uses the rel-

atively cheaper dumb bombs on lower profile targets on the kills lists. Digi-
tally-driven genocide is now being framed in the language of Big Tech eco-
nomics, as one Israeli intelligence officer puts it, "You won't want to waste
expensive bombs on unimportant people—it's very expensive for the country
and there's a shortage of bombs."[144]

A shortage of weapons but no shortage of Palestinian death. A mandate
against waste of dumb bombs, but digital kill lists to slaughter men, women,
and children in spectacularly efficient and inhuman fashion. Machines have
taken hold of the genocidal wheel, driving the siege in Gaza and this genocide, a digital genocide on both sides of the screen, to otherworldly stanzas
of human history. Technological advancement of war that has ushered in
downward spirals of Palestinian death, where inputting the masculine indictment of terror maximizes the desired output of prolific scales of collateral
death and predicted destruction. It is all by design, discursive and now digital
processes are buttressed with the new language of algorithms, inputs and outputs, kill lists and kill chains, dumb bombs and sophisticated killing machines

named "Lavender," "The Gospel," and the appropriately named and gendered, "Where's Daddy?"[145]

It all feels like a digital nightmare. Dystopian fiction from the pages of *1984* or the bleak screen of *Black Mirror*. But it is real, stunningly and inescapably so. Not even sleep or exile, or the temporary exile of sleep can liberate you from the nightmare of Gaza. Whether caught within its dragnet and the kill chain of names that makes death a predictive outcome, or on the opposite side of the world where that mobile phone pulsates and rings, opening up that digital Pandora's Box of gore that characterizes our new existence.

A digital nightmare, Gaza has become a "conveyor belt" of mass killing. One where death is no longer a human experience, but an outcome of a digital process where algorithms issue kill lists and orders, and machines wipe out human life with hyper-efficiency and without feeling.

Within this digital order of genocide, *feeling* is the final bastion of resistance.

## Finding Justice in Cape Town

*"The most potent weapon in the hands of the oppressor is the mind of the oppressed."*
— Stephen Bantu Biko, *Black Consciousness in South Africa*[146]

I landed in Cape Town thirty minutes short of midday and four days short of 250 days of genocide. I peered out of the window as the airplane descended onto the continent, and the country synonymous with apartheid.

I have been here before. My appointment as an "Extraordinary Professor" at the University of Western Cape's Desmond Tutu Centre made Cape Town a regular stop for me in recent years. But this was my first time in Cape Town since the beginning of the genocide in Gaza. Since the commencement

of a human catastrophe that made South Africa's history and its present focal in an urgent way.

The struggle against apartheid and genocide blurred into one in South Africa. So much so, that the nation assumed leadership against the latter within the International Court of Justice (ICJ) because of the former. Empathy fueled the South African case against Israel at the ICJ of genocidal acts. It propelled the nation that had defeated apartheid to make that *long walk toward freedom*, once again.[147] But this time, against the dehumanizing of another people.

South Africa's legal charge at the ICJ was coupled with a grassroots fight arising from Cape Town. In the colorful corridor of the city, Bo Kaap, pro-Palestinian murals were ubiquitous. Local artists, primarily of Cape Malay and Black descent, adorned the enclave's walls with pictures of iconic figures from Gaza, slogans proclaiming, "All Eyes on Rafah," and the Palestinian tricolor flag painted and projected even more prominently than the South African flag. In fact, the largest Palestinian flag in the world covered an entire apartment complex up in the hills of Bo Kaap, which sat high and overlooked the sublime Cape Town skyline below. These hills had eyes for Palestine.

I stood there, with friends, followers, and the artist himself, snapping pictures as I stepped foot in an entirely new world. This was not America, where statements of Palestinian solidarity were policed and demonized. This was South Africa, a hemisphere away and worlds apart, where South African history was bound closely to the Palestinian present. "We know what they are going through," shared Shakeel, a local. "This is what drives our union."

The young South African was focused on empathy. Yet, the word that took possession of me was emancipation. I was thinking primarily of the words of South Africa's most beloved native son, Steve Biko, and about how I was witnessing the "mind of the oppressed" being won back from the oppressor.

This is what freedom feels like, I thought. This is what a principled commitment to human dignity, civil rights, and the rule of law looks like. I pondered this as I stood in between an apartment complex shrouded with the Palestinian flag and the Cape Town skyline, while simultaneously standing on the shoulders of giants like Biko, Nelson Mandela, Desmond Tutu, and other South African freedom fighters who are the foundation for the fight rising from the halls of the ICJ and the hills of Bo Kaap today.

There we were, Arabs and Africans, on the furthest point of a massively colonized continent only days away from the bleak benchmark of 250 days of genocide. I reflected on the beginning days of that genocide, when the following words came to me before I posted them on Instagram:

*You know what also died in Gaza? The myth of western humanity and democracy.*

Places like South Africa, Colombia, Brazil, and nations rising from the so-called "Global South," are fighting for the humanity of the Palestinian people. They are, as brown and black peoples, filing cases and claiming principles that the *west* allegedly champions. But perhaps, just perhaps, the west only champions these principles for those who look and believe like them, or as Derrick Bell warns after the landmark *Brown v. Board of Education* case and the de jure demise of American apartheid, "converge[s] with their interests."[148]

Palestinians did not serve the interests of their Western masters. And echoing Biko, their collective mind refused the oppression and apartheid imposed by them. For them, the very act of survival was an act of resistance. Being alive in Gaza, as bombs rained down and ethnic cleansing reigned in, was revolutionary in and of itself.

As the siege in Gaza spiraled into a full-fledged genocide, the pristine façade of Western civilization began to decay before the world's eyes. The myth that the "West is modern, greater than the sum of its parts," and composed of the loftiest values and steered by the rule of law came crashing down.[149] The world was beginning to see the west as Cape Town did, as Bo Kaap had emblazoned with radiance across its colorful homes and halls.

From June 13th through June 18th, while genocide converged in what we in the Muslim faith observe as the holy slaughter of Eid Al-Adha and in the emboldened slaughter of civilians in Gaza, Cape Town was my home. It offered a break from the Islamophobia and hysteria of the United States, and its fires of authoritarian rage that silence dissent and crush student activism. The genocidal *fire this time* harkened memory of James Baldwin, who wrote, "[T]he terms 'civilized' and 'Christian' begin to have a very strange ring, particularly in the ears of those who have been judged to be neither civilized nor Christian."[150] I am an Arab and a Muslim, and like those Palestinian boys and men rounded up like sheep and pegged as terrorists, on American soil branded with the putative badge of terrorism on account of race, religion, gender, and ideas alone.

But in Cape Town, I am a man. An individual who, galvanized by the art on the walls in Bo Kaap, can speak my mind on Gaza. I can use ideas as weapons of truth, in solidarity with local "guardians of truth," a term assigned by another great Black thinker—Franz Fanon—who preceded Biko, Mandela, Tutu, and the South African leaders like Lee-Shae Udemans and

Naledi Pandor emerging today. Fanon embodied the intellectual living under colonization, and wrote about the responsibility of whoever holds that status to, "draw up a list of the bad old ways characteristic of the colonial world, and hasten to recall the goodness of the people, this people who have been made guardians of truth."[151]

I wish I could stay in Cape Town for another week, or month, surrounded by the warmth of newfound family and *Falasteen* radiating from every wall and alley. But it is time to leave, back to the belly of the beast where human rights are myths for Muslims and dignity deferred for Gazans.

I board my departing flight from Cape Town, empowered by meeting with survivors of apartheid committed to justice in Gaza. My return flight home to the United States transports me back to the sobering reality of realpolitik and American power. I sink into my seat, minutes later, recalling Franz Fanon's words in *Black Skin, White Masks*, written in the aftermath of a colonial apartheid that stretched across Africa, the Arab world, and pillaged places beyond and in between. He wrote, "I do not carry innocence to the point of believing that appeals to reason or to respect for human dignity can alter reality."[152]

Lost innocence is part and parcel of both intellectual life and life itself. As we age, if we are paying attention, we lose our innocence. But the loss of innocence should raise the commitment to fight oppression. If not by simply wanting to remake the world in the image of reason and human dignity, then for the sake of doing what's right. To be fully wed to principle, regardless of whether justice is realized in Gaza.

I found this in Cape Town. And am grateful to the city and its guardians of truth for modeling these things on the walls of Bo Kaap, the halls of the ICJ, and every place beyond and in between where Gaza and South Africa join hands and hearts.

## Searching for Edward

*"I am an Oriental, writing back at the Orientalists, who for so
long have thrived upon our silence."*
— Edward Said, *Out of Place*[153]

Edward Said, who died more than two decades ago, has been called many things—a literary critic and an exile, an unyielding voice for Palestinian self-determination, an educator, a trailblazer, and even "a prophet of the political violence" unfolding in the United States today, almost two decades after he took his final breath.

During a lifetime that spanned nearly sixty-eight years and witnessed definitive geopolitical currents and shifts, Said stood apart as one of the world's most incisive public intellectuals. A Palestinian by birth and an American by station, Said took on this role in the early 1980s, following the publication of *Orientalism*, a text that dismantled European misrepresentations of Islam in its annals of literature.

This moment converged with the aftermath of the Iranian hostage crisis and ascendance of the Islamic Republic of Iran, which reoriented the whole of Islam as the "enemy of the West." And, in turn, propelled Said and his work onto the center of the public stage.

There, seated in front of cameras and alongside intellectual contemporaries and adversaries, is where Said thrived. Debating and dissecting the day's political turbulences in corridors of power long monopolized by white men, is where Said —an exile who embodied the very marrow of the term—also revealed his genuine identity: a public intellectual of the highest order, fiercely loyal to ideas and ideas alone. Untethered to governments or organizations, professional entities or political parties that would disrupt that fidelity to his truth.

Said combined his life as an intellectual with an unbending commitment to advocacy. While an upstart professor at Columbia University in New York City in the late 1970s, he served as a member of the Palestinian National Council (PNC), an aberration from his refusal to enlist in organizations and bind himself to ideology. He remained a member of the Council until 1991, two years before Yasser Arafat and the Palestinian Liberation Organization (PLO) signed the Oslo Accords, a measure he emphatically denounced and famously called the "Palestinian Versailles"; not because he did not believe in peace or in dialogue, but because he thought Arafat had signed away virtually all key Palestinian demands and got precious little for Palestinians in return.

On the domestic front, Said was a staple voice for the American Arab Anti-Discrimination Committee (ADC), the largest Arab American civil rights organization, which provided him with a platform to analyze the crackdowns on Arabs' and Muslims' civil liberties that swelled in the 1990s and proliferated horrifically after 9/11.

In May of 2001, several months before the 9/11 terror attacks, Said debated noted contrarian Christopher Hitchens on the matter of Palestine. During their exchange, Said discussed his chance meeting with Israeli pianist and conductor Daniel Barenboim in a London hotel in 1994. In the lobby of that hotel, a Palestinian scholar readying to deliver a series of lectures for the BBC crossed paths with an Israeli musician preparing for his concert.

Said, an amateur musician himself, saw Barenboim for who he was instead of what the political order narrowly cast him to be.

That London hotel lobby became a crossroads where one might expect a Palestinian "firebrand" and an Israeli national to avoid one another or even to collide, but instead "a great friendship" began.

The two men spent the weekend together in London grappling with their differences through a shared love of music. And five years later, Said organized a concert for Barenboim at Bir Zeit University in the West Bank. It was one of the first times that an Israeli musician performed in the Palestinian territories.

Five hundred people jammed into the University's Kamal Nasir Hall that evening on January 29th, 1999. And for two hours, the oppressive shadow of warring peoples and the shrill perils it sounded were drowned out by the majesty of music.

This was orchestrated by Edward Said. An intellectual auteur whose unbending commitment to principle, most notably humanism and its staunch opposition to dogmas religious and secular, moved him to form iconoclastic bonds with mercurial minds like Hitchens; engage in tempered exchanges with Orientalists like Bernard Lewis; and pursue transformative friendships with Israeli musicians like Barenboim.

An exile in every measure, Said eschewed the comfortable landings of political dogma for the roaming freedom of complexity. He refused to be constrained by any one of his many identities, and furiously rebelled against any and all intellectual confines.

Said did so by remaining steadfastly committed to principle, and the matters that formed the core of his intellectual concerns: Palestinian self-determination; uncovering Islam beyond its Orientalist bind; and the humanism that ties the two.

Dogma on the Left all too often stakes a claim over a narrow plot of moral rectitude, at times appearing to punish those who explore past it. The Right does precisely the same, albeit, of course, with much more political weight and resources behind it: the hysteria around such terms as "critical theory" is designed to intimidate, not persuade.

Against this bleak, Flanders Fields-like landscape of entrenched and fortified positions, Said, a Palestinian American intellectual who defied binaries and extremes of all orders, still matters today.

Indeed, the irony of recent commentaries that peg Said as a "violent prophet" of unfolding movements reveals an ignorance of who he was, and the ways in which his work instructs us. Not only would Said reject the anti-intellectualism that flings an arrogant hand at free exchange and academic freedom, but he would rebel against it and fight to preserve these ideas.

Today, with few exceptions, pundits on the Left and Right engage in an ongoing vicious and vapid exchange of personal attacks. Attacks flare across a widening political divide, almost never meeting in between to debate. One can simply watch Fox, CNN, or Piers Morgan to see this on daily display.

Today, doing what Said did would be "platforming" an "enemy," to use a particular activist parlance. It's hard to imagine something like the debates between Said and Hitchens, who eventually and infamously became an advocate for the illegal War in Iraq, the War on Terror, and the "clash of civilizations" that undergirded both.[154] And the Manichean intellectual split of good vs. evil, prevalent in too many arenas, would never allow for the possibility of the Palestinian Said facilitating the Israeli Barenboim's musical performance in the West Bank, and the many conversations that followed. It would lobby against it and question the very friendship that spawned its coming into fruition as disloyal or subversive.

So many liberals and Leftists of today, if they had been in charge instead of Said, would have robbed an oppressed people of that elusive freedom cre-

ated by music. This might seem trivial and fanciful against the backdrop of the very real evils activists are fighting today. But music, culture, and intellectual engagement have a way of transforming reality that transcends and belies even the harshest material obstacles. Music roams beyond manmade boundaries drawn along disputed territories, and ideological boundaries drawn even more deeply in the minds; it allows connections and alliances to be made where even the most inspired polemical exchange can forge none.

Nothing of this is meant to suggest that Said wouldn't support something like the struggle for Black lives today in the U.S. Of course he would, and he would do so in strong terms. But if we paint Edward Said as a totem of anti-intellectual violence, we are committing an act of historical revisionism of which he was determined to so masterfully disarm with his pen. And even more persuasively, with his personal walk of life.

Said roved independently atop the widening schisms of dogma that quiet the symphonies of free exchange and swallow up those who dare to walk across that middle expanse, the territory that trenchant American thinker Sarah Kendzior calls "flyover country." This intellectual "flyover" terrain is where nuance is layered and rich, and complexity is given voice. A space that today's prevailing discourses fly past, but which Said was comfortable in, employing meticulous analysis and detail which is absent today.

Like music, Said—the exile who only found permanence in sanctuaries of principle and the public squares of intellectual engagement and exchange—roamed rebelliously in the face of the unheeding flag-waving that entraps us today, and which challenges the banal political discourses that pervade new mediums of "discourse."

In *Representations of the Intellectual,* Said reminds us that, "One task of the intellectual is the effort to break down the stereotypes and reductive categories that are so limiting to human thought and communication."[155] His voice and his leadership are needed now more than ever. In a world where so much is said and cowards leave too much unsaid, Said's words pour into voids that only his voice can fill.

As Gaza faces genocide, and public intellectualism dies alongside it, I find myself searching for Edward and his wisdom more than ever before.

## The People's Champ

If Gaza shows us one truth, it is that champions are made when given an opportunity to be seen and heard, not born as a consequence of race, religion, or ties to a dominant lineage. The colonial and genocidal lies of Orientalism, Islamophobia, racism, and their vile counterparts insist on the latter, but the fight of those afflicted by them tells a different story.

I never anticipated to find the fight against genocide at the Ultimate Fighting Championship (UFC), but that is where the world took the matter and me in July of 2024. It was a brisk early morning in Manchester, England, but the world was raging hotter over a genocide that extended into its ninth month. With my American and Canadian friends who made the trans-Atlantic trek, we filed toward the Coop Stadium in our keffiyeh's and FC Palestina football jerseys. We were among predominantly white English fight fans stumbling from the pub or from their beds, anxious to see the bout that would feature top Palestinian contender, Belal Muhammad.

Belal is a friend of mine, a proud Palestinian from "Little Palestine" in Chicago. Both of us are Midwestern kids with roots in the Middle East, wearing the black eyes of hard pasts from the latter, mixed with the gritty, blue-collar drive of the former. As he rose up the UFC ranks, Belal made the four-hour drive from the Windy City to Detroit, my hometown, to embrace the vibrant Arab and Muslim American community that saw a champion in him long before he lifted up UFC gold.

At first, the community embraced him for his words on Palestine more than for his actions within the Mixed Martial Arts (MMA) cage. Until the two harmonized sublimely as he claimed win, after win, over top-ranked adversaries in the UFC. Unlike most fighters, Belal wore the struggle for Palestine on his chest. Everything he did inside of the UFC cage, and beyond it, screamed Palestine. Our friendship formed in between the crossroads of activism and our kindred love for combat sports, and I proudly observed his climb up the ranks to vie for the welterweight UFC championship. I followed his rise, closely, and marveled at how he championed speaking up against the genocide more than his impressive string of ten straight victories inside the cage. Days before the bout, I reached out to Belal, who sent me a fight ticket to watch him make history in the U.K.

Any MMA fan is intimately aware of the racial feel of a UFC event. To paint the racial picture by way of orange-skinned example, Donald Trump is met with the biggest roars and applause when he enters the stadium during a fight card. The UFC experience is enthralling, but tinged for me by the feeling that a January 6th-style insurrection can pop off at any moment in the crowd. And this keeps those of us not part of the racial majority feeling perpetually on edge. I feel it particularly while draped in the colors of Palestine and while donning the checked keffiyeh that is perceived as a symbol of terrorism.

But if Belal could fight amid this hostile crowd, then we, his supporters, could survive the hot seats in the stands.

In no time, it was fight time. Belal's image took over the massive screen around the stadium and atop the cage, then his song rang out. *The song* of the moment filled the stadium so rebelliously, so resoundingly that it felt like all of Palestine was in the building; as if a different kind of protest was set to march forward, toward a different kind of capital or state structure of power that spelled support of the status quo. A structure of power which stated this song, the keffiyehs worn around the necks of fans in the stands, Palestinian flags waving and lifted up in the rafters, and the tangible spirit of Gaza, did not belong there. There were cold stares and confused looks of many alongside us silently echoing what we feared, but this was a different night. This was a new day when the counter-story of Gaza, and a novel chapter of a Palestinian champion would be written inside of that cage.

Not a cage where Palestinian men and boys were imprisoned, beaten, tortured, and raped, like its morbid counterparts in Gaza. But an athletic cage, where adversaries fought on equal footing and symmetrical levels. A cage where soldiers were not armed by foreign superpowers, fed steroids of military might that guaranteed a lopsided victory against a starved and emaciated adversary. This was an even fight. A dignified fight. A fight where the winner did not hide behind the impregnable steel of tanks, or the cowardly buttons of AI-driven killing machines. A fight of men, two men, who stared each other directly in the face the day before, stripped of everything except their pride, skill, and will.

This cage was a stage. Not a crucible. And on this morning in July, in the heart of a city where Mancunians sing songs called "Blue Moon" and "Don't Look Back in Anger," another tune bounced off the walls when Belal marched in draped in the red, black, green, and white of Palestine:

*Ana demmi Falesteeni!*
*Ana Demmi Falesteein!*

"My blood is Palestinian," the lyrics rolled in and bounced off the stadium walls so sublimely, so magnificently, affirming that victories were inevitable. The championship victory in the cage, and the grander triumph unfolding beyond it.

The song rang out as Belal stepped closer to the cage:

> *I belong to my people; I sacrifice my soul for them*
> *My blood is Palestinian, Palestinian, Palestinian*
> *My blood is Palestinian*
> *We stood for you, our homeland*
> *With our pride and Arabism.*[156]

The counter-story was being written, sung, and later, fought inside the cage and beyond its steel walls. Belal strode onto the canvas, marauded across it with the spirit of a warrior ready to represent his people, confident that his will would overpower the so-called "dominance" of his opponent, local product Leon Edwards. However, this moment in history was far bigger than Edwards or the adversaries beyond the cage. Muhammad—like "the greatest" boxer who shared his name—would shock the world with a counter-storybook ending that claimed victory for the whole of Gaza.

The fight was a forgone conclusion. Belal dominated the first round, then proceeded to drop Edwards on his head, maul and ragdoll him across the cage, and cruise toward a unanimous decision victory. Everybody in the crowd, except us, the Muhammad faithful, was shocked. Perhaps most among them was UFC President Dana White, who stepped into the cage with the Palestinian flag as the backdrop, to complete the ceremonial placement of the UFC welterweight championship belt around the waist of Muhammad. Days later, that snippet would be the most viewed UFC belt wrapping ever, another credit to the resounding global support for Gaza.

The moment was bigger than sport. It was a fight that represented an even bigger fight. Muhammad, moved by the weight of it all, dropped to his

knees in the familiar Islamic ritual to pray. He was not prey, like the legions of men in Gaza lined up and stripped down as terrorists. Muhammad was a champion, a world champion, who redeemed his blindfolded Palestinian brothers and redefined Palestinian masculine identity before the whole world inside a different cage in Manchester.

"Hearing Bruce Buffer announce 'And newwww...' at the end of it all was something I'll never forget. In its own way, it felt like a massive victory for the fight for liberation," shared Dr. Zayr Ahmed, a Pakistani Canadian who observed the fight two seats away from me, shortly after UFC boss Dana White strapped the championship belt around Muhammad's waist.[157]

If felt like far more than a victory limited to one bout, to sport, to a spectacle confined to a stadium in the north of England where race riots against Muslims and immigrants would break out in the coming days. This was a victory of the underdog, who rose from the lowest ranks of the UFC after being denied a title shot on account of his identity, on account of being unapologetic about his Arab Muslim masculinity and outspoken Palestinian identity. Talha Ahmed, who witnessed the event alongside me, shared,

> *Watching him become the first ever Palestinian UFC champion made me realize one thing: the heart and soul of the sport lie not only in the spectacle of combat but in the stories of the fighters who dare to dream and conquer. What a historical moment waving the Palestine flag in Coop Arena with friends and family of Belal.*[158]

Belal Muhammad offered a counter-story of redemption and remaking atop a different kind of canvas. The canvas of the UFC cage, where billions were forced to acknowledge the greatness of a Palestinian man who claimed gold against all odds, with his first words after claiming the title being, "The real fight is in Gaza, this is nothing."

He knew himself. Just like Edward Said and Mahmoud Darwish, Motaz Aziaza and Khaled Nabhan. Belal rewrote history by making it on his own terms, with the warrior's might of a fighter who wore the colors of Palestine around his shoulder and across his chest. A warrior who championed the cause against genocide amid the echoes of cowardly silence emanating from the likes of DJ Khaled, civil rights "leaders" who screamed "Me Too" and "Black Lives Matter" but went silent on Gaza, and the legions of loud-mouthed influencers reduced to mimes when confronted with the fear of losing brand deals and job opportunities. Belal's words made him a contender, but his actions for his people made him a champion.

Our world champion.

## When Phones are Bombs

*"Visibility is a trap."*
— Michel Foucault, *Discipline and Punish*

It was approaching one year. One year of genocide. What many initially believed would be a passing season of siege on Gaza extended and evolved into a whole calendar year of nonstop airstrikes and sinking nihilism.

This season of annihilation wasn't the same. And as days blurred into months, nothing was the same. Gaza, and the remnants of humanity swallowed by its crucible of hard truths, would never be the same.

On our screens we continued to take in images of the fresh massacres and fraught horizons of Gaza. And as October 7th came around again, a genocide that was now spilling into wars in the West Bank and Lebanon.

Mobile phones and cellular devices were portals to view the uncut images and unhinged evil of genocide. But after eleven months, they transformed into more than mere portals. The screens that kept us at an intimate distance as we witnessed annihilation, in hours, changed into something more sinister. Something far more cautionary, and in Lebanon, catastrophic.

My phone vibrated violently.

Text after text.

Notification after notification.

Phone call after phone call after phone call.

That device, that served as a double agent of disseminating information and signaling warning, pulsated with that familiar shake and shrill of looming menace.

I could feel the peril rush inside my body before my fingers tapped open the Pandora's Box of messages waiting for me early on Tuesday, September 17th, 2024.

I knew something was wrong before I knew everything that was awaiting me on that screen. The screen I stared at ritually, that dark screen where doomscrolling had replaced casual conversations with friends and check-ins with mothers, benign scrolls through social media timelines and banal strolls through online shops.

Cellular devices have mutated past their formative forms. Even more than just tools for communication, for those of us fixated on Gaza and its bloody spill into places nearby, they were telescreens of catastrophe. This morning, my eyes raced past the words on text and WhatsApp messages, stopping at images of blood spilled and scattered across ceramic floors, elderly women staring at hands missing fingers, children with mangled hands, mixed bandages, and overflooded hospital rooms.

This was not Gaza. This was Lebanon.

The portraits penetrating my screen and sending my phone into violent pulsation were not from Rafah or Deir al-Balah, but Beirut and Bint Jbeil.

"We are very scared, they are making our phones into bombs," my friend Abed texted, marking the first words I read on my screen, found between the horrific pictures that jumped from it. On Day 348 of the genocide, only weeks away from its grim one-year anniversary, the annihilation of Gaza exploded into Lebanon.

The very devices that drove us deeper into the digital genocide, and kept us trapped between the siege and our screens, had become something else. They were no longer barriers between us and Gaza, or bridges connecting us to its victims, they were *bombs*. The digital devices were bombs, that exploded in grocery stores and streets, bedrooms and school playgrounds across Beirut and the tiny nation-state of Lebanon.

The very hands and fingers we use to communicate with loved ones were blown off by thousands of exploding pagers in Lebanon, made in Taiwan but doctored by Israel. However, before the facts were fully known, hysteria subsumed the streets of Beirut and the imagination of Lebanese society.

*"Could our phones be made into bombs?"*

A Lebanese cousin of mine asked, echoing a question that reverberated, again and again, through the minds of millions in the Mediterranean nation and beyond it. The era of digital darkness, which had been ushered in in Gaza, plunged even deeper that third Tuesday of September, in that moment when mobile devices morphed into bombs.

That moment brought new meaning to the phrase, "my phone is blowing up." We were looking straight into a bleak future when mobile phones would become killing machines. "This was one of the greatest terror attacks of our time," shared Hassan Chami, a native of Dearborn, Michigan, home to a prominent Lebanese diaspora. He continued, "I'm not surprised that western media won't label it terrorism, which would undeniably be the case if the roles were reversed."

Orientalist proverbs converged with new world explosives. Human beings were walking time bombs. They were not just mere targets of lording tanks and "Lavender" drones, but roving explosives carrying the enemy's weapon within their palms and pockets. *If this is not terrorism, I don't know what is.* Those words rose to the fore of my head, as I learned about a three-year-old toddler, ten-year-old girl, and scores of elderly Lebanese civilians slain by the pager terror attack.

Yet, Western media outlets left out the word "terrorism" when reporting on the explosions, redacting it and its stark reality from coverage. Reporting that, as the days of genocide rolled toward an entire year and expanded into Lebanon, exposed itself as more noise than news, as more complicity than coverage.

The images of murdered children and grandmothers with mangled hands were more compelling than any *New York Times* headline or BBC byline. Their white noise and Western newsreels seemed to only find innocence in the civilian mirrors of Ukraine, while violently dispensing of any humanity owed to the children, mothers, and sons of Lebanon.

A Lebanon I knew very well. A Lebanon marred by woes and wars of the past that perpetually shadow its present. But those shadows on Tuesday

exploded into a day that would usher in tomorrows riddled by more airstrikes, more explosions, more death and more darkness.

I know that darkness very well.

I feel it seep through the screens as I read rambling messages from family members and hysterical voice notes from loved ones. Across that barrier of those digital devices which were now made into bombs. An idea so surreal, so morbid, that it seemed to belong to Hollywood film or Orwellian fiction.

Or . . . well . . . a reality that I had never imagined, had indeed arrived. The missing fingers on the hands of elders and the morbid images of murdered children signaled the coming of a new frontier of digital warmongering and mobile-phone massacres, where war crimes are inflicted by imported technologies and exploding pagers.

What may read like alarmism for some, sounded the alarm of millions on Tuesday, September 17th, the 348th day of genocide in Gaza and the 1st day of a new kind of digital war for the rest of the world.

Bassem Youssef, the Egyptian comedian who rose to new stages of fame

during the Gaza genocide, put it poignantly by way of a tweet:

> *And suddenly my phone, our*
> *security system, my kids' tablets are*
> *time bombs that detonate at the whims of one country. You win*
> *Israel. Not a single politician or late*
> *night show talks about this? None of*
> *that worth the news? Nothing*
> *"funny" come from out of it? The*
> *whole country is truly a hostage. The*
> *whole world is.*[159]

Youssef, who brought intellect and levity to a catastrophe, echoed the fear of millions in Lebanon, and billions beyond it who held onto their mobile phones and pagers, tablets and mobile devices with a new kind of fear. A new color of fright that superseded spying or surveillance, traversed past the paranoia of malware and passed by the fear of being doxed or canceled.

Fears of Big Brother were eclipsed by the doctored evils of phones made into bombs, and black mirrors turned into roving weapons.

The phone pulsated again, just as violently, a day later. On September 18th, as I boarded a plane for Wake Forest University to lecture on Islamophobia and anti-Semitism, word of walkie-talkies detonating in Lebanon exploded onto my screen.

More dead. Even more injured. After nearly a year of genocide, the numbers mattered less than the limitless absurdity of it all. An absurdity that ushered in a nihilism among friends and family members in a nation where war was imminent, and the airstrikes from American jets and explosions of Taiwanese technologies loomed in the days to come.

My plane landed. In those liminal moments between flying and landing, driving and stopping, I stared into that ticking timebomb in the palm of my hands where all five fingers still remained.

I stared, while stopped at a gas station somewhere between the airport and the elite American university, at hands less fortunate than mine, fingers blown off the still-growing hands of toddlers and the wrinkled appendages of elders. I witnessed those crying hysterically while crowded into hospital rooms where the presence of dead and dread overwhelmed the doctors.

Hours later, I lectured to a classroom of affluent children, the majority of them staunchly pro-Israel. Many of them voiced their rigid support of the state's war crimes against the Palestinian people of Gaza and parroted the banal platitudes of pro-genocide pundits. There I was, lecturing to blueblood students who were silver spoon-fed imperial misinformation that justified the mass killing of civilians and children. "Terrorists" and "human shields," they stated over and again, "collateral damage" and the propaganda that unsaw Palestinians as bona fide human beings.

The beat from Frank Ocean's "Super Rich Kids" drummed in my mind, and his lyrics about, "Too many white lies and white lines" sang in my head as scenes from Beirut crosscut with the faces before me, with every "red line" crossed and bombsite dotted.[160] I tried to teach them to find balance amid it all. On another surreal stage of the absurd theatre that was my life these past eleven months, I was teaching a legal treatise published in 2018 about anti-Semitism and Islamophobia that had renewed resonance in 2024.

This was hardly a pedagogy of the oppressed in Winston-Salem, but an Arab professor standing in front of a firing line. I stole moments in between the lecture and lessons and meetings to learn about the downward digital spiral in Lebanon.

My Lebanon, a nation that raised me as a child of war in the eighties and roared for my return today. I remember the screams of American fighters above our building on Verdun Street in the heart of Beirut, the sound of jets and sirens signaling coming bombs and the cries of neighbors when disaster struck.

I remember it all. And remembered it in stark detail as I stood before Ivy League audiences and affluent students spewing support for a genocide from the comfort of college desks. The perch of a digital dissonance had remade their mobile phones into echo chambers of hawkish zeal. Trapped inside hardened silos of groupthink where critical thought and empathy are shot down as the first victims.

My phone pulsated as I walked out of the classroom. I lifted it and held it further from my face than usual, moved by an irrational fear that was thoroughly rational for my family members in Lebanon, and read:

"What can I say, we hear booming sounds and rush to check on our family's safety. Because of what Israel is doing, the streets are empty, and people are scared. We live in constant fear," wrote my friend Abdallah Kobrolsi, a resident of Sidon in Lebanon.

In the next image I saw the face of a ten-year-old girl, Fatima, who looked a lot like my own niece who shared that very name. She was killed by the pager terror attack.

Then, my cousin wrote, and I read:

"I'm too afraid to use my phone, how if it explodes. How if it kills me?"

*How if it kills me?*

The words jumped from my screen. A mobile phone. A device designed in Silicon Valley, California pieced together somewhere in China or Taiwan, imported into Lebanon.

His question stuck in my head. They stung me there and everywhere else.

*How if it kills me?*

There I was. Alone in a distant college hallway, standing alone, in a world marred by a year of genocide in Gaza and marked by impending war in Lebanon.

Alone, in quiet hallway, with nobody around me and nothing but my mobile phone in hand.

A ticking time bomb.

A traveling target.

A mobile explosive.

A tethered weapon that walked with me, wherever I went.

*How if it kills me?*
*How if it kills me.*
*How if it kills me!*

His question morphed into a realization than alarming fear. The words rose and then rounded across my mind like a whirling dervish, entranced by the divine and stirred by his love for Him.

But this ritual was anything but holy.

It was wholly sinister.

Then, as soon as the words stopped suddenly in my head, the revelation came.

The real bombs Israel planted were not in the pagers or mobile devices carried across the streets and squares of Lebanon.

The real bombs were the explosive fears that they had planted in the minds of people everywhere. All of us, anywhere. The imminent and intimate fear that even our phones could made into bombs.

A thought so irrational, and once so unbelievable, until that fateful Tuesday in Lebanon when everything changed again. When everything changed for the 348th time on the 348th day of genocide, that bled into Lebanon, October, and an entire calendar year.

How if it kills me?

The words whirled in my head one last time as my body stood still.

In Wake Forest, for the first time in eleven months, I did what I could not do in the days before, between, and beyond this last day that felt like anything remotely normal.

I turned off my phone in the middle of the day. Disconnecting myself from Gaza, Lebanon, and everything I knew and everyone I loved.

I was not disconnecting myself from the world.

I was un-detonating a bomb.

Or, well, what had become a bomb for loved ones in Lebanon who would not see the tomorrow that waits for the rest of us.

A tomorrow that wades into one year of genocide in Gaza, a new war in Lebanon, and novel woes of a dystopic future when our bodies are walking time bombs.

## Conclusion

## Old Body, New Mind

*"I'm not supposed to be back here,*
*I've invaded our time.*
*Sucked me back like a vacuum.*
*To observe from a bird-eye... view."*
— Nemahsis, *Old Body, New Mind*[161]

Counter-stories may not always usher in new beginnings. Not at first, at least. But powerful narratives from the bottom can inspire action, instill hope, and open up new possibilities for the millions that hear and feel them. If there is a bright side to this genocide, the one that radiates most for me is witnessing the groundswell of solidarity and support for the women, children, and yes, the men of Gaza. This global groundswell is only possible because of the inroads, both terrestrial and digital, created for the natives of Gaza to make their stories and remake themselves in the eyes of the world.

Around the cities we live in and around the clock, these counter-stories have brought pain and horror. There is some hope and levity, at times, but more frequently there is anxiety, trauma, and alarm about a world where human life matters so little. A complexity of feelings that reflects the complexity of a people who have been flattened into cardboard caricatures and faceless terrorists for far too long. That alone marks progress away from the dominant narratives and toward a greater public understanding of who Palestinian men are, were, and strive to be. Dr. Ed Hasan, a Palestinian American living in Washington, DC who avidly followed the siege from a professional and personal vantage point, shared,

> *Witnessing Palestinians reclaim their narratives through digital media was both devastating and liberating. It was devastating because we've had to fight to be recognized as human, worthy of life, rather than being reduced to dehumanizing stereotypes of the "Other," perpetuated by the Orientalist lens. It was liberating because it empowered us to shatter Islamophobic tropes, reclaim our identity, and let our heart and soul shine, illuminating our true character that had long been suppressed.[162]*

While the death toll stated otherwise, the people of Gaza have been arguably winning the narrative war. And inarguably, the digital narrative war, as the online timelines and pages across social platforms have elevated the counter-stories of genocide at a frequency, and virality, that stamped out War on Terror myths. It is a new day, where the stories of besieged men and boys, women and children in Gaza are heard the world over. The once buried histories of downtrodden people made manifest in digital form—to be shared and reposted, retweeted and disseminated for billions to see in real time, right now.

Despite its myriad connections in Silicon Valley and billion-dollar allies, Israel has been losing the social media war more definitively than it has its wayward military campaign. Beyond the clear bias aligned platforms like Instagram has for Israel, the vile celebration of Palestinian death by Israeli soldiers and the nonstop barrage of morbid images from Gaza has created a "widespread campaign of sympathy" that dominates social media timelines.[163]

Unlike fading media outlets, like CNN or the BBC, the digital pages of social media are less corporatized, and far less vulnerable to commercial purchase. The Big Tech gatekeepers at the top can be bought, without question, but not all the users that populate their pages and platforms. Against dragnets of censorship and algorithms of suppression, the people moved by the digital counter-story of Gaza remain resolute, march across timelines, and mount protest after protest online. If powerful states, most notably the U.S. and Western European nations choose to remain on the left side of history, the people —real people—in nations all around the world have swiped left and stayed right. On the right side of history, that is.

———————

In her novel about the perils of Palestinian life under occupation, *Wild Thorns*, the novelist from Nablus, Sahar Khalifeh writes, "Sink in the mud, Palestine, and kiss the world goodbye."[164] The world has witnessed Gaza sink toward the hells of irreversible damage, destruction, and death, which will mar future generations with the stains of psychological injury and intercept the future of children slain far too soon. Khalifeh's words ring with a capitulation to the horrors inflicted on the land and people of Gaza, where legions of its natives bid that final "goodbye" through the genocide's theatre of displacement, dispossession, and death; never to return again.[165]

As a young boy living in war-torn Beirut, a child reared by war and its cruel hands, I was familiar with those perils. It was the late 1980s, and

Lebanon was gripped by the final stages of an existential unmaking. The Lebanese Civil War fractured the nation into unrecognizable parts, which made way for the very Israeli jets and occupying military that bludgeons Gaza today. That in late September of 2024, returned to Beirut and the south of Lebanon to drop the very same bombs that fell atop our heads decades ago. New bombs, old fears. Old feelings, new beginnings.

*New beginnings, ah*
*New beginnings, wake up akh*
*The sun's goin' down*
*Time to start your day, bruh.* [166]

*Nights* and nightmares. I can feel death creep in, in the air of night. Late nights then dark days.

The daze of genocide blurring days into unrecognizable sleepwalks. Through life, or pieces of a former life.

Marred by flour massacres and playgrounds turned into killing fields. Hospitals made into morgues. Lives cut short while electricity cut off to threaten newborn babies tethered to breathing machines grasping for that last bit of fuel. That last gasp of breath.

Six days into the siege, I was awake at 4 a.m. texting my friend Issam, a journalist in Lebanon. We exchanged messages, like we did before, with "stay safe my brother" being the last direct message I left in his box. It was marked "read" below the text, when I opened the DM at 9 a.m.. Yet, his life marked dead by a headline reading "Al Jazeera journalist Issam Abdallah assassinated."

Nights and nightmares.

Another morning of mourning, six days into genocide, that would be the first of an endless string of many in 2023 and 2024, bringing me back to 1987 and 1988. "Shooters killin' left and right, Workin' through your worst night," as nights fade into daze and days roll back into past memories. [167] Time during genocide moves differently.

And time brings us to new stations in life. New faces and phases, false wars and fresh wounds. Yet, these passages of life feel more like returns than novel encounters. There is an intimate familiarity to sieges on Gaza and assaults on Lebanon, to the mourning of slain family members and mornings made frantic by the nonstop messages about pager terror attacks.

New stations in life, colored by native faces and unnatural fears that define life in north Gaza and south Beirut, Rafah and Zeitoun. Old stations blur with fresh news as I write about Edward and Issam, Hind and Reem, Ali and Aaron, faces from present and past times that prominently color my worldview. These people are one, unseen and unheard, summoning me back to the very olive station where my father held my hand, and taught me about *us*.

*Gaza did sink.* It sinks deep into our souls. Rising sublime action, rooting new champions and rotting old dogmas. It sinks deep in pages of brave new histories and bolder generations that affirm, through written word and marching action that Gaza endures. We can never unsee what is within. Gaza has sunk into all of us.

*"You can cut all the flowers,*
*but you cannot keep Spring from coming."*
— Pablo Neruda

# ENDNOTES

## INTRODUCTION

1   Translation of the poem by Sinan Antoon, "Silence for Gaza," Mondoweiss (November 24, 2012).

2   Id.

3   I adopt the definition of genocide enshrined in the 1948 Convention on the Prevention and Punishment of the Crime of Genocide, widely called the "Genocide Convention," which the International Court of Justice (ICJ) adopts to litigate cases filed under its jurisdiction. Most notably, the case filed by the State of South Africa against the State of Israel on December 29, 2023. There are five types of genocidal acts outlined in the Genocide Convention: mass killing, causing serious bodily or mental harm; deliberate infliction of conditions of life calculated to bring about a group's destruction in whole or in part; imposing measures intending to prevent victim group birth; and forcible transferring of children from the group. The latter category was the lone one missing from the South African petition. See Noura Erekat and John Reynolds, "South Africa's Genocide Case is a Devastating Indictment of Israel's War on Gaza," Jacobin, p. 3 (Jan. 11, 2024). In order to prove these acts, the petitioning party must provide evidence of both genocidal intent and genocidal actions.

4   Using the phrase from Muneer Ahmed, in *A Rage Shared By Law: Post September 11 Racial Violence as Crimes of Passion*, California Law Review, Volume 92 (2004).

5   Khaled Beydoun official Instagram page, October 8, 2024, at @khaledbeydoun.

6   A leading definition is offered by the United Nations Convention on the Prevention and Punishment of the Crime of Genocide, Article II. This definition offers the following typology of genocide: "In the present Convention, genocide means any of the following acts committed with intent to destroy, in whole or in part, a national, ethnical, racial or religious group, as such: (a) Killing members of the group; (b) Causing serious bodily or mental harm to members of the group; (c) Deliberately inflicting on the group conditions of life calculated to bring about its physical destruction in whole or in part; (d) Imposing measures intended to prevent births within the group; (e) Forcibly transferring children of the group to another group." UN (1948).

7   Marc Lamont Hill and Michael Plitnick, *Except For Palestine: The Limits of Progressive Politics*, p. 119 (2021).

8   *Times of Israel* Staff, "UNRWA Review: Israel Hasn't Provided Evidence that Agency Staff Were Terror Group Members," *Times of Israel* (April 22, 2024).

9      Hill and Plitnick, supra note 7, at p. 150.

10     Quoting Teju Cole, who stated, "Writing as writing. Writing as righting. Writing as rioting. On the best days, all three." See Aarik Danielson, "Power to the Poets," *Columbia Daily Tribune* (Feb. 1, 2019), citing Cole's viral tweet and its words.

11     Instagram page (@khaledbeydoun), posted on October 8, 2023.

12     Homage to Achebe's brilliant novel, *Things Fall Apart* (1958).

13     The village, Bint Jbeil, translated into "daughter of the mountains" (Arabic).

14     Edward Said, *Representations of the Intellectual*, p. xvii (1994).

## Before Day 1

15     Edward Said, *Orientalism* p. 86 (1978).

16     The population of Gaza has been estimated to be between 2 and 2.3 million, with real figures becoming more undeterminable after the siege. See "Gaza Strip, Statistics and Facts," Statista (Jan. 30, 2024).

17     A "Panopticon" is form of prison designed to maintain continual surveillance of the captives, with an all-seeing watchtower in the center that stands as a metaphor for the omniscient state. Jeremy Bentham, *Panopticon* 60–64 (1791).

18     "The society of subjugation is a type of surveillance society in which the State wields surveillance technology to form a policing architecture designed to police, persecute, and then stamp out an oppositional minority group. Through an ensemble of punishment, discipline, and control, the State administers digital surveillance tools," in conjunction with other mechanisms of practical and military force, as illustrated by Israeli relationship vis-à-vis Gaza. Khaled A. Beydoun, *The New State of Surveillance: Societies of Subjugation,* 79 Wash. & Lee L. Rev. 798 (2022).

19     *Orientalism*, supra note 15, at p. 86.

20     Elia Zuriek, "Strategies of Surveillance: The Israeli Gaze," *66 Jerusalem Quarterly* p. 31 (2016).

21     Id at 21.

22     Michel Foucault, *Discipline and Punishment: The Birth of a Prison* p. 203 (1975).

23     Id.

24     Id at p. 119 (2021).

25     Michelle Nichols, "UN Accuses Israel of Denying Gaza Aid Access as Famine Takes Hold," Reuters (May 5, 2024).

26     Restrictions against "cruel and unusual punishments." U.S. Const. *amend*. XIV.

## Day 7

27    Aime Cesaire, *Discourse on Colonialism*, p. 44 (2001).

28    An earlier version of this article was originally published in the *Harvard Law Review*, Volume 136 (2022).

29    Jean Paul Sartre, *Colonialism and Neocolonialism*, p. 75 (2001).

30    Khaled A. Beydoun, *The New Crusades: Islamophobia and the Global War on Muslims*, p. 5-13 (2023).

31    Cesaire, supra note 27, at 52.

32    Ian Haney Lopez, *White By Law: The Legal Construction of Race*, p. 9 (1996).

33    Leti Volpp, "The Citizen and the Terrorist," *UCLA Law Review*, Volume 49, pp. 1575-1576 (2002).

34    Caroline Mala Corbin, "Terrorists Are Always Muslim But Never White: At the Intersection of Critical Race Theory and Propaganda," *Fordham Law Review*, Volume 86, p. 455 (2017).

35    "Racialization" is defined as the process of extending racial meaning—itself "an unstable and 'decentered' complex of social meanings constantly being transformed by political struggle" assigned to identities in society. Michael Omi and Howard Winant, *Racial Formation in the United States*, p. 110 (2015).

36    Richard Delgado and Jean Stefancic, *Critical Race Theory: An Introduction*, pp. 2-3 (2001).

37    Khaled A. Beydoun, "Islamophobia: Toward a Legal Theory and Framework," *Columbia Law Review*, Volume 116 (2015), which offers a definition of Islamophobia rooted in law that assigns the indictment of presumptive terrorism onto Muslims.

38    Cesaire, supra note 27, at p. 59.

## Day 10

39    Discussion with Abed Ayoub at the Headquarters of the American Arab Anti-Discrimination Committee (ADC), in Washington, DC, on October 27, 2023.

40    Abed Ayoub and Khaled Beydoun, "Executive Disorder: The Muslim Ban, Emergency Advocacy, and the Fires Next Time," *The Michigan Journal of Race and Law*, Volume 22, pp. 215-217 (2017).

41    Discussion with Abed Ayoub at the Headquarters of the American Arab Anti-Discrimination Committee (ADC), in Washington, DC, on October 27, 2023.

42    "Suspect in Death of 6-Year-Old Palestinian-American Boy Was Obsessed With Israel-Hamas War, Prosecutors Say," NBC News (October 16, 2023).

43    Leti Volpp, "Citizenship Undone," *Fordham Law Review*, Volume 75 (2007).

44    This question became ubiquitous on and off media, and most prominently asked on shows like *Piers Morgan Uncensored.*

45    Khaled A. Beydoun, Acting Muslim, *Harvard Civil Rights and Civil Liberties Law Review,* Volume 53 (2018).

46    Fatema Mernissi, *Scheherazade Goes West: Different Cultures, Different Harems,* p. 114 (2001).

47    Benjamin Netanyahu likened the two groups, although dramatically different on a range of fronts, merely on account of their Muslim identities. "Hamas is ISIS and ISIS is Hamas," Netanyahu famously stated after October 7th. Ishaan Tharoor, "Israel Says Hamas is ISIS, But it is Not," *The Washington Post* (October 25, 2023).

48    Khaled A. Beydoun, American Islamophobia: Understanding the Roots and Rise of Fear (2018).

49    Carl Jung, *Memories, Dreams, Reflections,* p. 112 (1962).

50    This essay was originally published in CNN, on October 21, 2023.

## Day 16

51    Gil Scott Heron, "The Revolution Will Not Be Televised," *Pieces of a Man* (1971).

52    Shoshana Zuboff, *The Age of Surveillance Capitalism: The Fight For a Human Future at the New Frontier of Power,* p. 67 (2019).

53    A Netflix original series (2011).

54    Andrew Guthrie Ferguson, *The Rise of Big Data Policing: Surveillance, Race, and the Future of Law Enforcement,* p. 2 (2017).

## Day 34

55    Edward Said, *Representations of the Intellectual,* p. 47 (1994).

56    A tribute to the classic novel by Ghassan Kanafani, *Men in the Sun* (1963).

57    Marndan Barghouti, *I Saw Ramallah* (1997).

58    Sahar Khalifeh, *Wild Thorns,* p. 66 (1991).

## Day 50

59    The technical definition of terrorism is comprised of two elements. Namely, violent action that is conducted in the name of a particular political ideology. However, since the War on Terror, the term has been conflated intimately with Arab and Muslim identity, giving the label a deeply racial form and resonance that diverges from its technical, facially neutral legal definition.

60    Medical apartheid refers to a system where access to healthcare and medical resources is inequitable, often based on race, socioeconomic status, or geography, creating stark

disparities in health outcomes. In Gaza, medical apartheid manifests as restricted access to essential healthcare services due to blockades, limited resources, and strategic bombing, exacerbating health disparities and as the siege rolled onward, foreclosing emergency medical care to accosted victims.

61    Staff, Israeli Minister Supports "Voluntary Migration" of Palestinians in Gaza, Al Jazeera English (November 14, 2023).

62    Khalifeh, supra note 58, at p. 56.

## Day 51

63    Jomana Karadsheh, Florence Davee-Attlee, and Abeer Salman, "Palestinian Man Grieves For 3-Year-Old Granddaughter as She Slept in Gaza," CNN (Nov. 29, 2023).

64    A neighborhood in central Gaza.

65    Grandfather (Arabic).

66    Karadsheh, supra note 63, at p. 1.

67    Id.

68    Soul of My Soul, at p. 1.

69    Id.

70    Karadsheh, supra note 63, at p. 1.

71    Id.

72    "Palestinians Pray in Ruins of Gaza Mosque Destroyed by Israel," TRT (Apr. 3, 2024).

## Day 60

73    Katya Adler and Toby Luckhurst, "Macron Calls on Israel to Stop Killing Women and Babies," BBC (Nov. 10, 2023).

74    Nadda Osman and Aina J. Khan, "Israel-Palestine: Civilian Palestinian Men Stripped and Detained by Israeli Army," Middle East Eye (December 7, 2023).

75    Osman and Khan, supra note 74, at pp. 1-2.

76    Friday is Islam's holy day, where men and women convene at mosques for collective prayer. Attending Friday prayer at the mosque is compulsory for men.

77    President George W. Bush in the immediate wake of 9/11 explicated that the War on Terror was "global." See Khaled A. Beydoun, "Exporting Islamophobia in the Global War on Terror, Vol. 95 *NYU Law Review Online*, pp. 81-83 (2020). See also Khaled A. Beydoun, " New Crusades: Islamophobia and the Global War on Muslims" (2023), where this thesis was applied to additional case studies, including Israel and Palestine.

78    "Following Shocking Testimonies of Israeli Killings and Field Executions of Palestinians in

Gaza, the Red Cross Must Step Up to Fulfill Its Obligations," Euro-Med Human Rights Monitor (Dec. 20, 2023).

79    See Muneer I. Ahmad, "A Rage Shared by Law: Post-September 11 Racial Violence as Crimes of Passion," Vol. 92 California Law Review, pp. 1259 (2004). Ahmed writes, "A desire for vengeance found broad support among the American public, and ultimately found expression in American foreign policy." Id at p. 1300.

80    Referencing Kimberlé Crenshaw's theory of "intersectionality." See "Mapping the Margins: Intersectionality, Identity Politics, and Violence Against Women of Color," Vol. 43 *Stanford Law Review*, pp. 1241, 1244-45 (1991).

81    "We are fighting human animals, and we act accordingly," Israeli Defense Minister Yoav Gallant said as he announced a "complete siege" on Gaza on October 9, 2023. Sanjana Karanth, "Israeli Defense Minister Announces Siege on Gaza to Fight 'Human Animals,'" *Huffington Post* (Oct. 9, 2023).

82    Mike Brest, "Israel Admits Viral Photos of Stripped Detained Palestinian Men 'Should Not Have Been Taken:'" US, Wash. Examiner (Dec. 13, 2023).

83    Richard Delgado, "Storytelling for Oppositionists and Others: A Plea for Narrative," Vol. 87 Michigan Law Review, p. 2411 (1989).

84    A British miniseries featured first on Channel 4 in the U.K. then Netflix, that highlights the role of technology in shaping a dystopian future. The six-season miniseries was first televised in 2011.

85    Brest, supra note 82, at pp. 1-3.

86    George Orwell, *1984* (1949).

87    See Chapter 1, Part II.

88    Edward Said, *Out of Place: A Memoir* (2000).

89    Khaled A. Beydoun and Nura Sediqe, "Unveiling: The Law of Gendered Islamophobia," *California Law Review*, Vol. 111 (2022).

90    Deepa Kumar, *Islamophobia and the Politics of Empire: 20 Years After 9/11*, p. 6 (2021).

91    Tia Goldenberg, "Harsh Israeli Rhetoric Becomes Central to South Africa's Genocide Case," AP (January 18, 2024).

92    Todd H. Green, *Presumed Guilty: Why We Shouldn't Ask Muslim Men to Condemn Terrorism* (2018).

93    "Orientalism had strong gendered dimensions, and the era also saw the development of colonial feminism, that is, feminism weaponized to serve empire." Kumar, supra note 90, at p. 20.

94    The Abu Ghraib torture camps were Iraqi prisons operated by the U.S. military during the Iraq War. In 2004, reports and images emerged revealing systematic abuse

and torture of detainees by U.S. personnel, including physical and psychological mistreatment, sparking widespread condemnation and investigations into human rights violations.

## DAY 64

95   Ruha Benjamin, *Race After Technology*, pp. 6 (2019).

96   Safiya Noble, *Algorithms of Oppression: How Search Engines Reinforce Racism* (2018). Noble also emerged into a vocal advocate against the genocide, using her platform as a UCLA professor to condemn it and the violent crackdown on students at the Los Angeles campus.

97   Cathy O'Neill, *Weapons of Mass Destruction: How Big Data Increases Inequality and Threatens Democracy*, pp. 3 (2016).

98   Staff, "Resignation in Israeli Military Trigger Domino Effect," IRNA (April 23, 2024).

## DAY 72

99   Federica Marsi and Ruwaida Amer, "Gaza Christians Fear 'Threat of Extinction' Amid Israel War," Al Jazeera English (November 10, 2023).

100  Id.

101  Id.

102  Fifi's family members were evacuated in March of 2024, and have relocated outside of the country.

103  Marsi and Amer, supra note 99, at p. 3.

## DAY 108

104  James Baldwin, *The Fire Next Time*, p. 5 (1962).

105  Instagram post from Motaz Azaiza from October 23, 2023, at @motazazaiza on Instagram.

106  Orwell, supra note 86, at p. 30.

107  Id.

108  Barghouti, supra note 57, at p. 182.

109  Instagram Post by Motaz Azaiza, supra note 105.

110  Thaslim a Begum, "Photojournalist Motaz Azaiza," *The Guardian* (February 16, 2024).

111  Zaina Arafat, "Witnessing Gaza Through My Instagram Feed," *New York Times Magazine* (November 20, 2023).

112  "[W]hen we hear 'terrorist,' we unconsciously associate it with all manner of

information, including, as it so happens, brown and Muslim perpetrators," and indeed, Palestinians in Gaza and beyond. Corbin, supra note 34, p. 464.

## DAY 136

113  *Palestine's Children: Returning to Haifa and Other Stories* p. 33 (2000).

114  Khaled A. Beydoun, *The Fire This Time*, Pen>Sword (February 27, 2024).

115  Id.

116  Sarah Khalil, Mohamed Bouazizi, *1984-2011: The Fire that Lit the Arab Spring*, *The New Arab* (December 17, 2020).

## DAY 152

117  Lisa Schlein, "WHO: Gaza Cut Off From Food, Water, 'Anything Which is Necessary For Any Sort of Life,'" Voice of America (VOA) (December 8, 2023).

118  Staff, "UN Says Israel Has Not Provided Proof of Allegations that UNRWA Staff in Gaza Belongs to Terror Groups," *Haaretz* (April 23, 2024).

119  Staff, "ICJ Ruling: Key Takeaways From the Court Decision in Israel Genocide Case," Reuters (January 26, 2024).

120  Kaamil Ahmed, "'Everything Beautiful Has Been Destroyed': Palestinians Mourn a City in Tatters," *The Guardian* (February 4, 2024).

## DAY 225

121  Featuring Anees, MC Abdul, and Amer Zahr (2024).

122  Staff, "'Heinous Massacre': Israel's Attack on Rafah Tent Camp Widely Condemned," *Al Jazeera English* (May 27, 2024).

123  Pointing to the popular Netflix television series, which "offers a vivid reflection on the social dimensions of technology – where we are and where we might be going with just a few more clicks in the same direction." Benjamin, supra note 95, at p. 70.

124  Adi Armon, "How Netanyahu's Father Adopted the View of Arabs as Savages," *Haaretz* (July 5, 2018).

125  Featuring Anees, MC Abdul, and Amer Zahr (2024).

## DAY 232

126  Barghouti, supra note 57, at p. 180.

127  Orwell, supra note 86, at p. 27.

128  Barghouti, supra note 57, at pp. 162-163.

129   Yuval Abraham, "'Lavender:' The AI Machine Directing Israel's Bombing Spree in Gaza," *+972 Magazine* (Apr. 3, 2024).

130   Nas, "N.Y. State of Mind," *Illmatic,* Columbia Records (1994).

131   Simon Frankel Pratt, "Israel's New Algorithmic Killing of Palestinians Sets Dangerous New Precedent," *Foreign Policy* (May 2, 2024).

132   Halil Ibrahim Medet, "Israel Paints Palestinians as 'Animals' to Legitimize War Crimes: Israeli Scholar," *Andalou Agency* (October 24, 2023).

133   Sigal Samuel, "Some Say AI Will Make War More Humane. Israel's War in Gaza Shows the Opposite," *Vox* (May 8, 2024).

134   Samuel, supra note 133, at p. 5.

135   Samuel, supra note 133, at p. 2.

136   Noble, supra note 96, at p. 10.

137   Abraham, supra note 129, at p. 2.

138   Id at p. 3.

139   Id.

140   Id at p. 5.

141   Id at p. 15.

142   Id at p. 10.

143   "[T]he Army routinely made the active choice to bomb suspected militants when inside civilian households from which no military activity took place. This choice, they said, reflected the way Israel's system of mass surveillance in Gaza is designed." Id at p. 20.

144   Id at p. 5.

145   "Additional automated systems, including one called "Where's Daddy?" . . . were used specifically to track and targeted individuals and carry out bombings when they had entered their family's residences." Id at p. 3.

## DAY 248

146   Steve Biko, *Black Consciousness in South Africa* (1978).

147   The title of Nelson Mandela's autobiography, published in 1995.

148   Derrick Bell, "*Brown v. Board of Education* and the Interest Convergence Dilemma," *Harvard Law Review,* Volume 93, p. 518 (1980).

149   Edward Said, *Covering Islam: How the Media and the Experts Determine How We See the Rest of the World,* p. 10 (1981).

150   James Baldwin, *The Fire Next Time,* p. 52 (1963).

151     Franz Fanon, *Wretched of the Earth*, p. 158 (1963).

152     Franz Fanon, *Black Skin, White Masks*, p. 224 (1967).

## Day 271

153     Edward Said, *Out of Place: A Memoir* (2000).

154     Khaled A. Beydoun, *American Islamophobia: Understanding the Roots and Rise of Fear*, pp. 78-82 (2018).

155     Edward Said, *Representations of the Intellectual*, p. xi (1994).

## Day 294

156     Ana Demmi Falesteeni, Mohammad Assal (2015)

157     Interview with Dr. Zayr Ahmed (Aug. 13, 2024).

158     Interview with Talha Ahmed (Aug. 13, 2024).

## Day 348

159     Tweet on X from Bassem Youssef, @byoussef, on September 17, 2024.

160     Channel Orange (Def Jam, 2012).

## Conclusion

161     Edward Said, *Out of Place: A Memoir* (2000).

162     Interview with Dr. Ed Hasan, on August 10, 2024.

163     Hatem El Zein & Ali Abusalam, *Social Media and War on Gaza* (2015). "Although it is difficult to measure the level of impact or success of war on social media on the conflict… the broadcasted images and videos can play a role in enticing sympathy with the victims." Id at p. 116.

164     Sahar Khalifeh, *Wild Thorns* p. 57 (1989).

165     Id.

166     Frank Ocean, *Nights, Blonde* (2016).

167     Id.

MOHAMMED EL-KHODARA OF NORTH GAZA